Please return/renew this item by the last date shown

**Herefordshire
Libraries**

**Herefordshire
Council**

HANDMADE FOR BABY

First Published in the UK in 2015 by
Apple Press
74-77 White Lion Street
London N1 9PF
UK
www.apple-press.com

10 9 8 7 6 5 4 3 2 1

Manufactured in China

ISBN: 978-1-84543-577-6

Publisher: Mark Searle
Commissioning Editor: Jacqueline Ford
Editor: Cath Senker
Assistant Editor: Tamsin Richardson
Layout: Emily Gregory and Michelle Rowlandson
Cover design: Michelle Rowlandson
Illustrations: Rob Brandt

Cover image credits
Front cover (clockwise from top left): Owl and tree decal by Patchi Cancado of TrendyPeas; Fabric blocks by Delia Randall of Delia Creates; Crochet teether rings by Aimee Trombetto of Apple n Amos; Memory keepsake box by Audrey Smit of This Little Street

Back cover (top to bottom): Pillow doll by Michelle Kreussel of the Fox in the Attic; Reversible baby quilt by Kelly Grooters of Petunias by Kelly; First birthday crown by Lainie Wicks of Maker*Land.

HANDMADE FOR BABY

25 Keepsakes to Create with Love

Charlotte Rivers & Emily Gregory

Table of Contents

Introduction

The arrival of a new baby is not only a cause for celebration, but also the perfect opportunity to get creative. After all, what better gift to give to that special little person in your life than something handmade? Whether you are making a gift for your own baby, or for a friend or relative's new arrival, this book features a wide range of different craft projects to suit all skill levels, and covers numerous craft types.

Each project has been created exclusively for the book by a specially selected group of some of the best-known crafters and makers from around the world. With years of experience and an abundance of creative talent as designers and makers, their ideas and contributions are an inspiration in their own right. From wall decals to a crochet blanket, quilt and first-birthday crown, we have made sure that all the projects that they have created for you are easy and achievable, giving you the opportunity to make something genuinely special for that small person in your life.

We have divided the book into five chapters: Announcements & nursery decorations, Preparing for the arrival, Welcoming the baby, One month old and First birthday, so you can choose to craft a gift that is appropriate for a particular age or occasion. There are 27 step-by-step projects included in the book as well as a special pregnancy-announcement photoshoot inspiration spread, with hints and tips on how to create a special announcement image. Each tutorial features handpainted watercolour illustrations to help guide you through the step-by-step process involved in making each item. We have included tutorials that will give you the opportunity to try your hand at a refreshingly diverse range of different crafts, including paper-based projects, sewing, knitting, crochet, lino-cutting and printing, painting, quilting and many more besides.

The practitioners whom we worked with to create the tutorials have kept the beginner crafter in mind at all times, yet you will be able to make such things as a beautiful felted mobile by Allyssa Zemke of Olive & Birch, a pair of stylish yet practical hand-painted storage buckets by Jessica Kelly of Hello Milky, a sure-to-be-loved keepsake memory box by Audrey Smit of This Little Street, some fun and playful fabric blocks created by Delia Randall of Delia Creates, using fabulous contrasting Skinny LaMinx fabrics, and hand-stamped leggings by Zeena Shah of Heart Zeena, amongst others.

Templates are provided where applicable, and we have also included inspiration galleries at the end of each chapter. These showcase a selection of projects by different practitioners that highlight the fantastic results that can be achieved with different craft techniques, materials, use of colour and alternative approaches. If you need to enlarge or reduce the size of a template, you can do this using a photocopier to scale it up or down as needed.

Compared with mass-produced shop bought items, toys and clothes that have been lovingly made by hand are always so much more special, and many are still cherished long after little ones have grown up. With a wealth of inspiration and practical advice for new parents, friends, family and crafters of all kinds, we hope you enjoy making the keepsakes that you will find in this book, and we're sure that if you do, they will be treasured for many years to come.

Happy crafting!

Charlotte Rivers and Emily Gregory

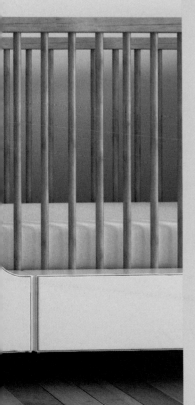

CHAPTER 1
ANNOUNCEMENTS & NURSERY DECORATIONS

Pregnancy-announcement photoshoot

Starting a family is an amazing experience, and pregnancy-announcement photographs are a great way of sharing your excitement with friends and family. There are many interesting and creative ways to announce your news, and the shoot itself can be a lot of fun. Not only will you be able to send the finished shots to your loved ones, but you will also have a great keepsake for your new family. The following pages aim to inspire you and give you some ideas for styling and shooting a photograph of your new or expanding family. Simple and stylish, all these ideas are easy to achieve with a few props and can be a really effective way to tell the world your good news.

It is important to get the light and timing right for your shoot. This photo by Amber Dixon of Three Bees Photography was taken about 15 minutes before sunset, when the light was perfect. A chalkboard hanging from the tree displaying this couple's chosen message is a simple yet beautiful way to announce a pregnancy. The board can say whatever you want, such as 'It's a Boy' or 'Expected June 2015'.

This self-portrait by photographer Ami Kochendorfer shows her obviously pregnant belly in silhouette form with an older (pet) sibling looking on adoringly.

Top tips for an announcement shoot

· Take your photographs outside if you can. This will give your images great light and make for pretty backgrounds.

· The best time to shoot outside is between 4 pm and 6 pm, or a little earlier if it is winter. This is known as the 'golden hour' – the light helps create beautiful, soft portraits.

· If you prefer to shoot indoors, try to use natural lighting if possible; positioning yourself by a large window is best.

· Think about how you can personalise your shoot. Take inspiration from the ideas shown here, but consider what is special or unique to your family and find a way to incorporate it into the shoot.

· Think about what creative skills you have that could be put to good use. For instance, do you have a talent for hand lettering?

· If you want to include your bump, the best time to shoot is between 30 and 36 weeks. Any earlier and you won't have a significant bump; any later, you may miss the opportunity if you go into labour early. You might also be too uncomfortable to enjoy the experience.

Including the other siblings in the photograph is a lovely way to introduce a new member of the family at the same time as conveying the sense of excitement (or emotion) that they feel about the new arrival. This photograph by Kensie Lee Photography uses simple blackboards to highlight the not-quite-here-yet fifth sibling.

Felted mobile

Crafter and maker Allyssa Zemke of Salt Lake City, Utah, USA, designs and makes beautiful typographic illustrated prints for her company Olive & Birch. Here she shows us how to make a colourful felted elephant mobile that will brighten up any nursery space. This is fun and easy to make, and once you've made this one you could create your own designs and make them for your own children or as gifts.

TEMPLATE

YOU WILL NEED

- Tracing paper
- Pencil
- 0.25 m (¼ yd) of grey felt
- Scissors
- Scraps of patterned or coloured fabrics
- Assorted embroidery threads to match the fabric scraps
- Grey embroidery thread
- Black embroidery thread
- Needle
- Polyester fibrefill
- Chopstick or knitting needle
- 12 to 14 wool felt balls (choose colours that will match your fabric scraps)
- Wire hanging mobile (we used a deconstructed hanging photo mobile)

CRAFT TIME

- 3–4 hours

Scaled down to 90% of actual size

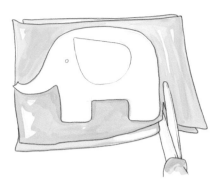

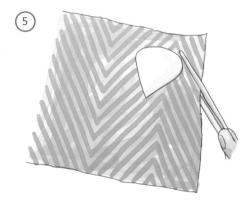

1. Enlarge, trace and cut out the elephant template so it measures around 9–10 cm (3½–4 in) wide. Be sure to make the ear white as you'll need to cut this out as a template later.

2. Cut out two pieces of felt measuring 12.5 x 12.5 cm (5 x 5 in), place the elephant template over both of them, and carefully cut out around the elephant shape.

3. Repeat this four more times so you have five elephants, each with two pieces, for the front and back.

4. Cut out the ear from the elephant template.

5. Place the ear template over two layers of scrap fabric and cut out carefully.

6. Repeat this step with the different scrap fabrics so you have five ears, each with two pieces each.

14

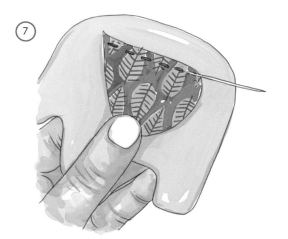

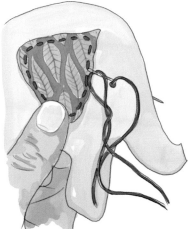

7. Place one ear piece on one side of an elephant and hand-sew using matching embroidery thread. You can use a basic running stitch; the stitches don't have to be very close together.

8. Repeat this on the other side of the elephant. Make sure you sew the ear on so that it is a mirror image of the first one.

9. Sew the ears on all the felt elephants.

10. To create the eye, bring the needle up from the back, tie two or three knots as if you were tying off at the end, then push the needle back down through the front, very close to the eye. Tie it off at the back. Repeat for the other eye.

11. Make eyes for all five elephants.

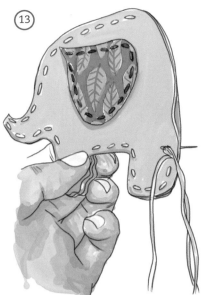

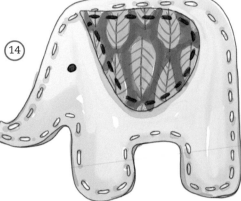

12. Now you need to sew the sides of each elephant together using grey embroidery thread. To make sure you don't leave any starting or ending threads exposed, start on the inside of the elephant. Tuck the threads inside the elephant. You will end the seam in the same way.

13. Using running stitch, sew around the edge of the elephant. Stop about 5 cm (2 in) before reaching the end.

14. Stuff the elephants with polyester fibrefill so they are loosely filled. Be sure to get the stuffing into the legs and as far as you can down into the trunk, using a chopstick or knitting needle. Then finish sewing the two sides together.

15. Repeat Steps 12 to 14 until all the elephants are stuffed and sewed.

16. String the elephants and wool felt balls together using grey embroidery thread. To begin, lay them out, allowing for each strand to have one elephant and two to four felt balls. Cut five pieces of thread 45.5–56 cm (18–22 in) long. Thread your needle with a piece of thread, tie a knot and push the needle through the centre of a ball. Tie another knot close to the top of the ball. Tie a further knot 7.5 cm (3 in) up the thread and then push the needle through the centre of an elephant. Again, tie a knot close to the top of your elephant. Add two more balls to that strand using knots to keep them in place. Repeat on the other four strands.

17. Tie each strand on to the wire mobile. Make sure that strands on opposite sides of each other have the same number of balls so that they balance.

18. Tie a long strand of embroidery thread to the top for hanging.

Bear cushion

Michelle Kreussel from St Leonards-on-Sea in East Sussex, is known for the cushions, dolls and embroidery crafts she creates for The Fox in the Attic. This bear cushion uses neutral colours that would suit any nursery and be both practical and decorative. The bear is adorable on its own or nested in amongst other animal-cushion friends.

YOU WILL NEED

- 2 x pieces of fabric 30 cm (12 in) square (natural, unbleached linen was used here)
- 4 x pieces of wool felt in different colours
- Air-erasable pen
- Optional: lightbox
- Scissors
- Embroidery hoop
- Embroidery needle
- Embroidery thread in colours to coordinate with the pieces of wool felt
- Pins
- Hand-sewing needle and thread (or sewing machine)
- Chopstick or knitting needle
- Polyester fibrefill

CRAFT TIME

- 5 hours

TEMPLATE

Scaled down to 50% of actual size

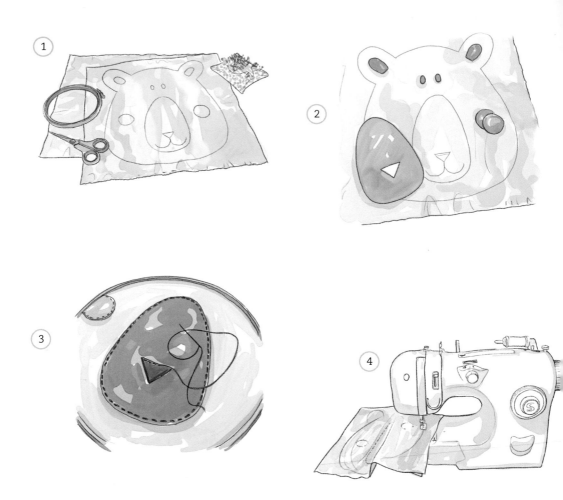

1. Enlarge and trace the bear template provided onto the right side of one piece of fabric using an air-erasable pen. It's useful to draw over a lightbox if you're using dark fabric, but with a lighter fabric you won't need one. Make sure to trace the same line on the wrong side of the fabric because you will need to sew on this line.

2. Cut out the shapes from the felt for the features. Place the fabric in the embroidery hoop to keep it taut.

3. Embroider the felt features on to the right side of the face of the bear. Use running stitch to sew on the ears, cheeks and nose, and embroider the mouth in backstitch.

4. Place the right sides of the fabric together and pin. Sew together with a sewing machine, or use running stitch if sewing by hand. Leave a 7.5-cm (3-in) gap in the side of the bear for stuffing.

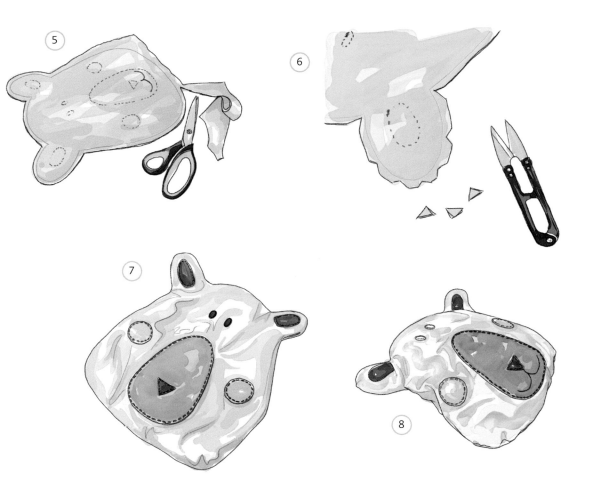

5. Cut around the outline of the bear, leaving a 1.3-cm (½-in) gap between the outline and the cutting line.

6. Cut out little triangles all around the edge of the bear. This will help to ensure the fabric does not pull when you stuff it. Be careful not to cut over the sewing line.

7. Turn the bear right side out. Use a chopstick or knitting needle to push out the fabric in the corners and other narrow areas, such as the ears.

8. Stuff the bear well with polyester fibrefill. Then hand-sew the gap closed, using hemming stitch.

Woodland-themed wall decals

Jana Kloučková Kudrnová is a graphic designer, illustrator and blogger living in the woods near Olomouc in the Czech Republic. Inspired by her surroundings, here she shows us how to create a removable decal woodland scene for a nursery, using templates featuring her illustrations (see pages 24–5). Removable wall decals are a great way of decorating a nursery – they are more affordable than wallpaper and they offer countless opportunities for customising designs using a variety of shapes and colours. They are also easy to make.

YOU WILL NEED

- Photocopier
- Pencil (3B+)
- Tracing paper
- Self-adhesive sticky back plastic (2 colours)
- Scissors
- Nail scissors
- Reusable adhesive

CRAFT TIME

- 1-2 hours

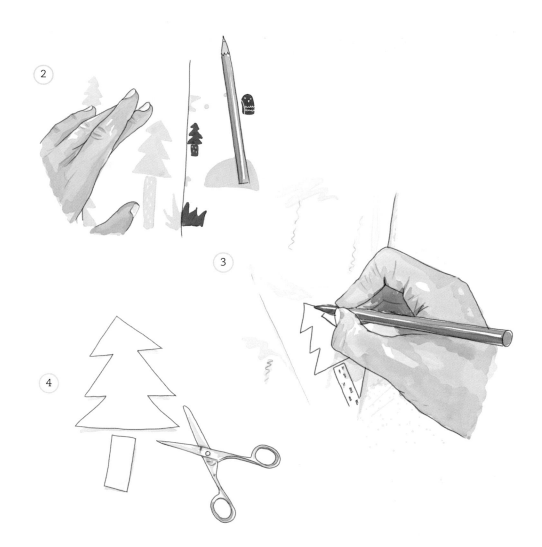

1. Enlarge the template to the size you want using a photocopier. For this tutorial, the template (see pages 24–5) was enlarged by 100% and 225%, but you can adjust the size as you like.

2. Using tracing paper and a pencil, trace around the different shapes one by one.

3. Place the tracing paper pencil side down on the back of the contact paper and draw over the lines. This will transfer your pencil marks on to the contact paper.

4. Use scissors to cut around all the traced images. Use nail scissors to cut out small details.

5. Arrange the whole scene on the wall using reusable adhesive to be sure you are happy with the layout. Then peel off the sticky-back plastic backing to stick the images on to the wall.

HELLO

BE BRAVE

ABCDEFGHIJKLMNOPQRSTUVWXYZ

HOOT

Colourful rainbow bunting

Mandy Pellegrin, a talented crafter from Nashville,
Tennessee, runs Fabric Paper Glue. She creates all sorts
of handmade goodies for the home, for parties and as
gifts. Here she shows us how to make some pretty bunting
for a baby's nursery. She has used a selection of beautiful
and bright Ann Kelle fabrics.

1. Cut out two triangles for each bunting flag. For each triangle, first cut out a rectangle 20.5 cm (8 in) wide by 23 cm (9 in) tall. Find the mid-point of one of the 20.5-cm (8-in) sides and cut diagonally from each of the corners of the opposite 20.5 cm (8 in) side to that mid-point. For this tutorial, we will make a bunting 264 cm (104 in) long using 12 flags, so in total you should cut out 24 pieces of fabric.

2. To create each bunting flag, place two matching pieces of fabric together, with the right sides facing. Sew the two angled edges together using a running stitch approximately 6 mm (¼ in) from the edge; this gives you the seam allowance.

3. Clip the seam allowance off at the tip.

4. Turn the flags right side out, and press with an iron.

5. Repeat Steps 2 to 4 for each of your 12 flags.

6. Measure out 264 cm (104 in) of double-fold bias tape, which will allow for 25.5 cm (10 in) of free tape at either end for hanging up your bunting.

7. Leaving the first 25.5 cm (10 in) free, place the top, unsewn edge of your first flag inside the fold of the tape. Sew together using a running stitch if hand-sewing or a straight stitch on a machine.

8. Repeat for all 12 of your flags. Use the free tape at each end to secure your bunting.

27

Hand-painted storage bucket

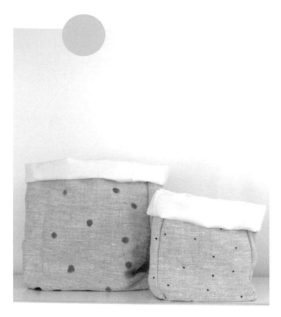

Jessica Kelly of Melbourne, Australia, runs Hello Milky, where she hand-prints and makes beautiful homewares, including cushion covers and toddler bedding. Here she shows us how to make a storage bucket for a nursery. These little buckets can be filled with just about anything: toys, creams, hats, booties, clothes, blocks. Just remember, the heavier the fabric you use, the stronger the bucket will be. If using something like a quilting-weight cotton, we recommend pairing it with canvas for the lining. Of course, you can make the bucket without painting your own fabric.

YOU WILL NEED

For the large bucket:
- Lining: Four 26.5 x 19-cm (10½ x 7½-in) pieces of cotton canvas (or equally heavy fabric) and one 19 x 19-cm (7½ x 7½-in) square of cotton canvas (or equally heavy fabric)
- Outer: Four 26.5 x 19-cm (10½ x 7-in) pieces of contrasting fabric (we used hand-painted 100% linen) and one 19 x 19-cm (7½ x 7½-in) square

For the small bucket:
- Lining: Four 24 x 15-cm (9½ x 6-in) pieces of cotton canvas (or equally heavy fabric) and one 15 x 15-cm (6 x 6-in) square of cotton canvas (or equally heavy fabric)
- Outer: Four 24 x 15-cm (9½ x 6-in) pieces of contrasting fabric (we used hand-painted 100% linen) and one 15 x 15-cm (6 x 6-in) square

For both sacks:
- Fabric paints or fabric-marker pens
- Cotton bud
- Pins
- Hand-sewing needle and thread (or sewing machine)
- Scissors

CRAFT TIME

- 2–3 hours

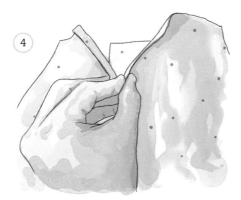

1. Set aside the pieces of fabric that will form the lining and paint your outer fabric. We have created a polka-dot pattern by dipping a cotton bud into fabric paint and applying evenly spaced dots to the four rectangular pieces of fabric. Alternatively, you can use fabric-marker pens. Allow the fabric to dry.

2. Once dry, take two of the outer panels, and lay one on top of the other vertically, right sides together. If sewing by hand, use backstitch and if using a machine, use straight stitch to sew down the right side 6 mm (¼ in) in from the edge to join the two together.

3. Take another piece of outer fabric and follow the same process, and then sew on the fourth piece, ensuring all the seams are on the same side.

4. Join the left and right panels, 6 mm (¼ in) from the edge, using the same stitch, to create a square.

NOTE

These instructions are for the large bucket, but the same method is applied to create the smaller bucket.

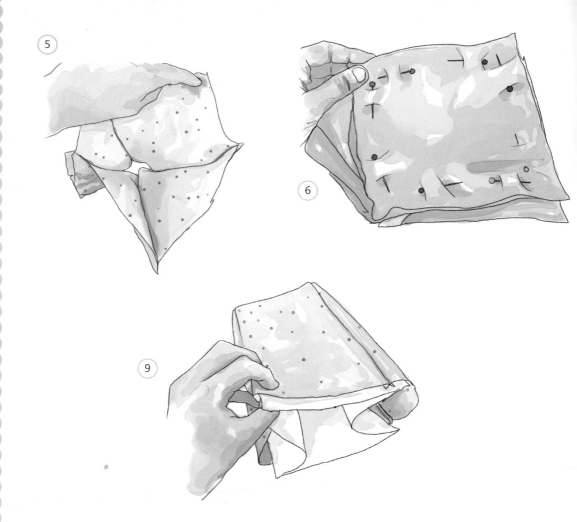

5. Open out the panels to create a square shape.

6. Take the base square of fabric and pin each side to the panels of the box.

7. Sew backstitch (or straight stitch) on the first side of the base, 6 mm (¼ in) from edge, removing the pins as you go. Do the same for the remaining three sides. Turn it the right way out.

8. Follow the same process to make the lining of the bucket. Make sure you sew the seams on the reverse side of the fabric.

9. Take the lining (with the seams facing out) and slip it into the outer bucket, lining up the panel seams. Pin around the top.

10. Sew backstitch (or straight stitch) around the top of the outer and lining buckets, 6 m (¼ in) from the top edge. Use blanket or whip stitch (or zigzag stitch on a machine) to sew around the raw edge to help prevent it from fraying.

11. Fold the top edge over once, by about 1 cm (⅜ in), then fold over again to the height that you would like your bucket to be. You can roll it over several times if you prefer that look.

Inspiration gallery

Top: This cheery hot-air balloon baby mobile, with matching bunting, was created using wool-blend felt by Cindy Taylor of Taylored Whimsey.

Above: Handmade in Paris by Laura Jane, this 'Pioupiou' cushion has been made with cotton velvet and makes a lovely addition to a nursery.

Right: This 'Choose your own Adventure' mobile, created by Madeleine Sargent of Made by Mosey, is based on imaginative play and uses different stuffed fabric shapes to create a story.

Top: These cushion dolls by Pink NouNou are double sided. The back has a fairytale printed on it, and the front features original illustrations of the main characters in the story.

Above: The patterned fabric for this storage bucket by Emma Collett of Splendid Love was lovingly screenprinted by hand. Collett uses organic, natural fabrics to make the buckets strong and durable.

Left: Shelly Hickmann of Lemon Tree Studio made scalloped bunting. The fabrics are gender neutral and feature Ann Kelle's Remix and Izzy Fabrics, and Robert Kaufman's Kona solids.

CHAPTER 2
PREPARING FOR
THE ARRIVAL

Chevron baby quilt

Crystal Motes is a crafter and maker who blogs at Stitched by Crystal. Here she shows us how to make a chevron quilt using a number of different patterned fabrics. Quilting is a great way to use up fabric scraps if you have some, or you can select new fabrics. Quilts also make lovely personalised presents that last for years.

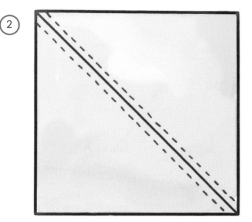

②

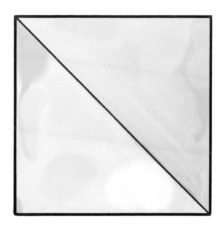

④

Cutting the fabric

For the quilt front, cut each of the assorted fabrics into 6 squares that are 18 x 18 cm (7 x 7 in). For the quilt binding, cut fabric into 4 strips that are 7.5 cm (3 in) wide × width of fabric.

Sewing

All seams are sewn with a straight stitch (machine) or running stitch (by hand). They are sewn using a 6-mm (¼-in) seam allowance unless otherwise noted.

1. Separate your fabrics into piles. In one pile put three squares of fabric A and three of fabric B. In the next pile put three of B and three of C. Continue separating in this fashion until you have seven piles. Your last pile should contain three squares of fabric G and three squares of fabric A.

2. Starting with your AB pile, place one A square and one B square right sides together. With a ruler, draw a diagonal line from one corner to the opposite corner. Sew along both sides of the line, 6 mm (¼ in) away from it.

3. Repeat Step 2 with the other four squares in that pile. Repeat these steps with the squares in the six other piles.

4. Cut along the diagonal line you drew to create two squares, and press the seam open. Repeat for all of the squares.

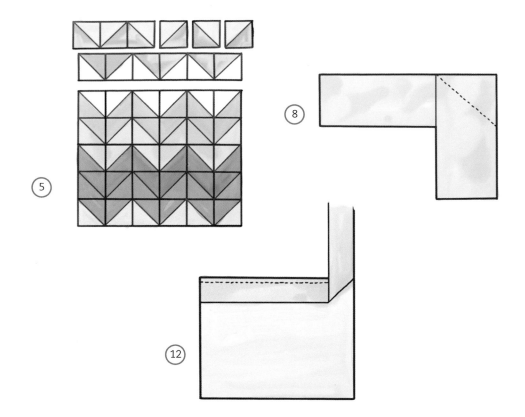

5. Sew the squares into strips. Then sew the strips together to form the quilt top, as shown in the placement diagram, lining up the seams in each row.

6. Lay the backing fabric out on a flat surface with the wrong side up and place the wadding on top. Centre the quilt top, right side up, on top of the wadding. Secure all three layers by basting or with safety pins.

7. Quilt by sewing through all three layers either by hand or with a sewing machine. Trim all raw edges even.

8. Place two of the binding fabric strips right sides together at a 90-degree angle from each other. Sew a diagonal line to attach them.

9. Trim the seam allowance and press the seam open. Repeat to add the other binding fabric strips to create one long strip. Press the strip in half lengthwise, with wrong sides together.

10. Starting about 20 cm (8 in) from the end of the bias strip, sew the raw edge of the strip along the raw edge of the quilt with a 1.3-cm (½-in) seam allowance.

11. When you get to the corner, stop sewing 1.3 cm (½ in) from the edge of the quilt and backstitch.

12. Flip the binding strip straight up and then fold it down along the edge of the quilt on the other side of the corner.

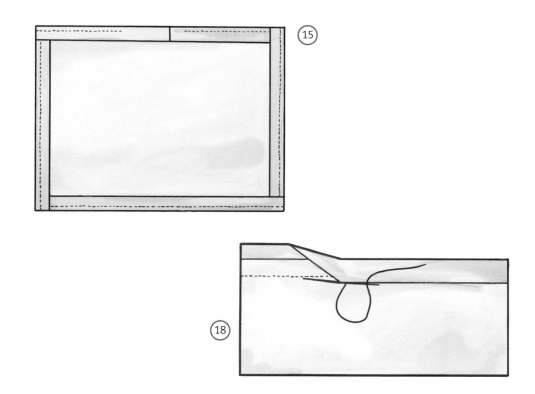

13. Begin sewing again at the very edge of the quilt.

14. Repeat Steps 12 and 13 for the other 3 corners.

15. Stop sewing when you get about 20 cm (8 in) from where you started. Lay the quilt flat and trim the binding strips so they overlap just 1.3 cm (½ in).

16. Unfold the ends of the binding strips and sew them together with a 6-mm (¼-in) seam allowance.

17. Finish sewing the binding to the quilt.

18. Fold the binding up and over the edge of the quilt and press. Sew the edge of the binding to the back of the quilt with a slipstitch.

Gnome hat

★

YOU WILL NEED

- 70-cm (27½-in) length
  of 1-m (39¼-in)-wide
  fabric, such as wool
  or another fabric that
  does not fray easily
  (do not use felt, as it is
  too rough for babies)
- Water-soluble pen
- Ruler
- Scissors
- Hand-sewing needle
  and thread (or
  sewing machine)
- Hook-and-loop
  fastener

CRAFT TIME

- 3 hours
  (1 hour using a
  sewing machine)

Based in Monterrey, Mexico, Llevo el Invierno is run by
Eri Flores, a crafter and mother of two. Through her blog
she shares tutorials about how to make a range of items
including children's accessories, costumes, clothing and
toys. Here she shows us how to make a little gnome hat
that will fit a baby aged 0 to 3 months. This hat makes
a great gift for a newborn as it fits a range of sizes.

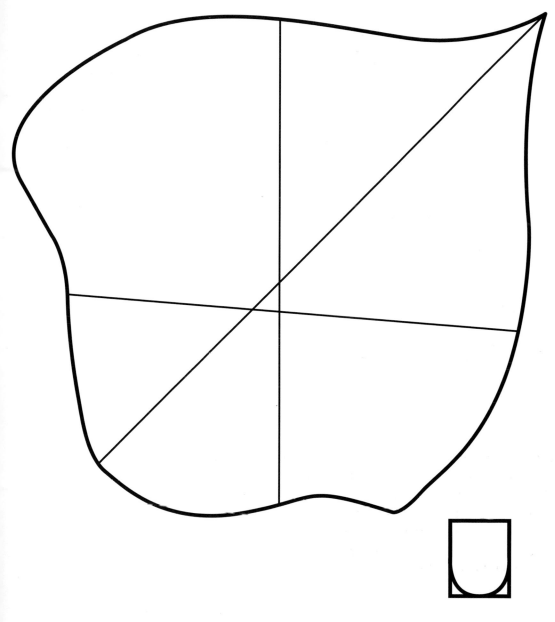

Scaled down to 70% of actual size

1. Enlarge and place the hat template on top of the fabric and draw around it in pen. Repeat so you have two shapes drawn out. Draw a second line 1 cm (⅜ in) away from the first lines, except on the bottom section. This gives your seam allowance. Mark the front and back of each section of the hat with an F and a B so you can remember which side is which when you start sewing. Cut out the pieces.

2. Draw a grid on the remaining fabric with rectangles 2.5 cm (1 in) wide by 3.2 cm (1¼ in) high. Draw about 12 strips, each of which should contain 12 shapes, giving you a total of 144.

3. Draw a letter 'U' on the bottom half of each of the shapes.

4. Cut the grid into strips, cut each strip into the rectangles, then cut around the 'U' in the bottom half of each shape so that you have a pile of scallop shapes. Use very sharp scissors so that you get neat edges.

NOTE

If you are sewing the hat using a machine, skip Step 5. You will sew your hat pieces together at a later stage.

5. Place the two hat pieces right sides together and sew around the first line that you marked out in Step 1.

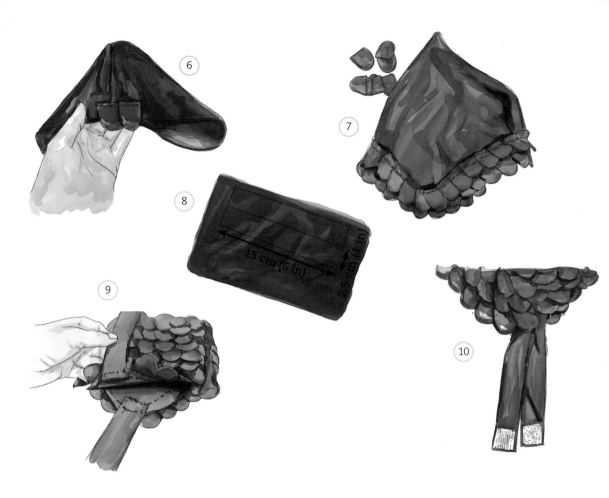

6. Turn the hat the right way out to sew on the first line of scallop shapes. Stitch each one around 6 mm (¼ in) from the straight edge top using backstitch. Sewing machine users: you will still be working with the two unsewn pieces of hat fabric so there is no need to turn the hat the right way. Use straight stich on your machine.

7. Repeat this procedure again, layering the next line of scallop shapes on to your hat so that they overlap the first line. Continue until you have covered the hat with scallop shapes.

8. Mark out two strips of fabric measuring 2.5 x 15 cm (1 x 6 in) and cut them out.

9. Using a needle and thread, sew one strip on to each side of the inside of the hat. Make sure that both straps are sewn on securely.

10. Cut a section of hook-and-loop fastener measuring 2 x 2 cm (¾ x ¾ in) and sew one piece on to the end of one strap, and the second piece on to the end of the other strap.

NOTE

If you are using a sewing machine, sew the two hat pieces together after Step 7. Place one top of one another, scallop sides together, and sew around the first line that you marked out in Step 1 using straight stitch.

Keepsake memory box

Originally from France, Audrey Smit of This Little Street shares her time between blogging and creating, and taking care of her girls at home. She loves colour, and here she shows us how to turn a vintage suitcase into a keepsake memory box that can be created and treasured for years. This is a place for first outfits, hand prints, favourite books, first drawings, pictures and much-loved toys. The memory box is a super-versatile project that can be made both with a vintage suitcase or a newly bought one, depending on what you can find.

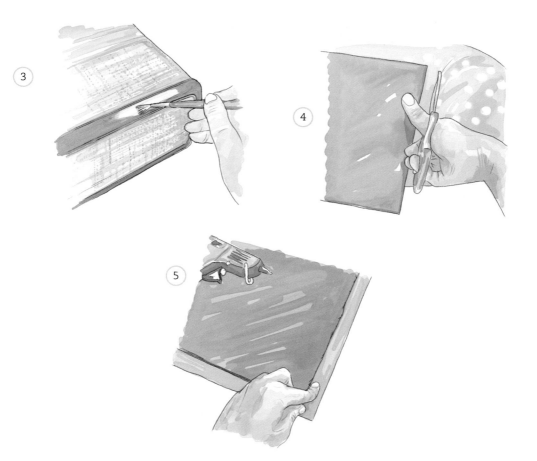

1. Pull out the lining of the suitcase. It is usually glued to a thick paper or card backing. If it is in good condition, you can cover it with fabric and reuse it, but if it is in poor condition, use it as a template to create a new lining. Cut out card pieces the same size as each part of the inside lining.

2. Clean the suitcase to remove any dust, dirt or old glue.

3. Paint any part of the suitcase that you will not cover with new lining, both inside and outside, including the handle. You might like to leave some of the vintage details as I did. Give the paint a couple of days to dry.

4. Organise and lay out the old lining pieces (or card pieces) on the fabric. Make sure the fabric is face down and that there is a least 2.5 cm (1 in) of fabric around each piece. Outline each piece with a pencil, then cut each piece 2.5 cm (1 in) away from the pencilled line.

5. Glue the fabric with a hot-glue gun onto the edges of the old lining/new card pieces, making sure the fabric is still face down.

TIP

Remember to paint around the tiny details of the suitcase and the places where the covering will stop. It will help to hide any places where the covering is not perfectly cut.

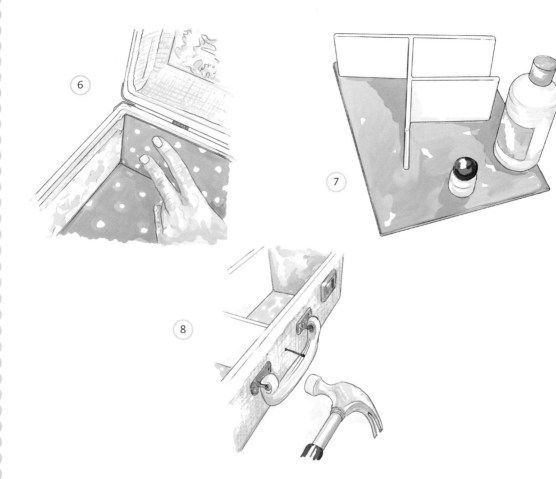

6. Hot glue each piece of fabric-covered card in its appropriate spot inside the suitcase. Start with the inside edges, then the base, and finish with the lid.

7. Make the insert. This particular suitcase has four compartments, but you could make as many or as few as you need. Draw the shape of the insert, then measure the inside of your box to figure out how long each piece of wood needs to be. Cut out each wooden piece. If you are not comfortable doing this, your local DIY shop will certainly be able to do it if you give them the measurements. Make sure the wood inserts fit correctly in the suitcase. Nail the pieces of wood together to create the insert.

8. Place the insert inside your suitcase, and nail it through the suitcase so that it will stay in place. The nails will not show once you cover up the outside of the suitcase.

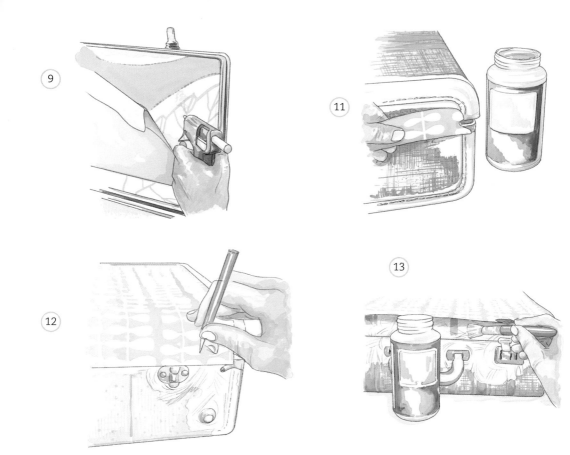

9. Use hot glue to stick the plastic envelope to the newly lined lid piece.

10. Take the fine paper or vinyl fabric, and cut pieces that will be roughly the size of each piece you will need to cover the outside of the suitcase.

11. Work one piece at a time. Place the piece on your suitcase and use a sharp knife to trim it so that it will fit snugly.

12. Make holes where needed for details such as the handle.

13. Using white glue, attach each piece of paper or fabric to the outside of the case.

TIP

If your lid piece is not snug enough for you to glue the envelope on to it, use a couple of staples to hold it in place. The staples will not show once the envelope is glued on top.

Baby shower decorative garland

Rae Anne Spence of Alpine Ridge Events in Port Angeles, Washington, creates an array of party decorations, with a strong focus on homeliness, for her business. Here she shows us how to create a 1.8-m (6-ft) garland made of various fabric strips. You could make it your own by adding vintage buttons or floral details, or even by cutting the bottoms of the tassels at an angle. The colour palette can be varied to make it more gender specific if you prefer. The garland will look equally beautiful as a backdrop to a buffet table or as an entrance hanging.

YOU WILL NEED

- 1.8 m (2 yd) fabric in any colour or pattern you choose (the garland shown uses 6 different kinds of fabric)
- Scissors
- Measuring tape
- Jute twine
- 2 chairs

CRAFT TIME

- 1–2 hours

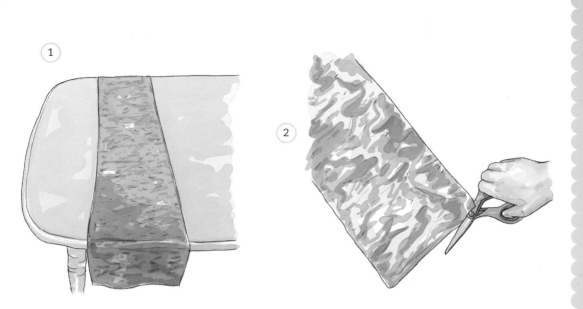

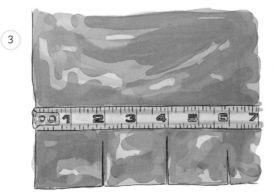

1. Lay the fabric out flat, and fold in half lengthways.

2. Cut along the fold to make two pieces of equal size. Pin the two pieces together.

3. Using the measuring tape, cut a small slit every 5 cm (2 in). Then go back and cut along the slits to create 5-cm (2-in) strips of fabric. You will have two strips for each cut because you have two pieces of fabric pinned together. Repeat this step for each of the fabrics you are using (if you are using more than one).

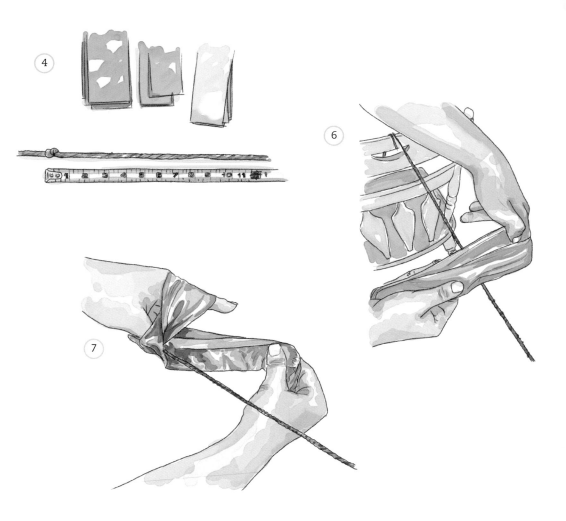

4. Measure two pieces of jute twine 2.4 m (8 ft) long. You will use 1.8 m (6 ft) for the garland, leaving 30 cm (12 in) at either end for hanging. Tie a small knot 30 cm (12 in) away from each end.

5. Tie the ends of the twine to the two chairs.

6. Take a strip of fabric, fold it in half, then place the loop of the fabric 5cm (2 in) over the top of the twine.

7. Hold the two ends of the fabric around the twine, then pull the loose end through the loop.

50

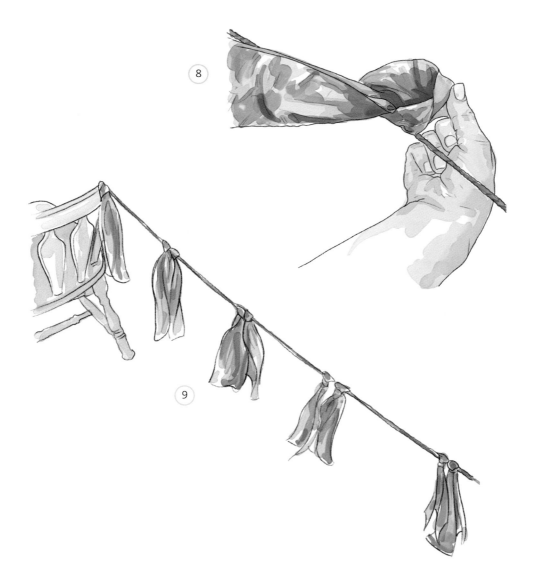

8. Pull the loose end tight to form a knot.

9. Tie on strips of the same fabric every 10–15 cm (4–6 in) along the twine. If you have more than six different fabrics, allow more space between the strips. Repeat Steps 6 to 9 for each fabric.

10. Use leftover strips of fabric to fill any gaps.

Knitted booties

Courtney Spainhower is the crafter and pattern designer behind Pink Brutus Knits, based in Indianapolis, USA. She has been designing knits since 2009 and is now also a knitting instructor. She initally started out designing mostly for children, but currently designs for men, women and children alike. Her patterns can be found in *Interweave Knits*, *Knitscene* and *Creative Knitting* magazines, as well as online in Holla Knits. Here she shows us how to create a pair of booties that can be made for sizes 0–3, 3–6, 6–9 and 9–12 months.

NOTE

If you are a beginner knitter, you can find out how to do the stitches on pages 128–33, and find a list of abbreviations on page 138.

YOU WILL NEED

- Rowan, Baby Merino Silk DK 66% Superwash Wool, 34% Silk (135 m/147 yd per 50-g ball):; 1 x 50-g ball in #679 Clay Alternative colours: 1 x 50-g ball in #681 Zinc (A); 1 x 50-g ball in #687 Strawberry (B); 1 x 50-g ball in #671 Straw (C)
- 4-mm (size 6) knitting needles
- Tapestry needle
- Leather laces, yarn or ribbon for tying that measures 35.5 [40.5, 40.5, 45.5] cm (14 [16, 16, 18] in)

CRAFT TIME

- 3–4 hours

CUFFS (MAKE TWO)

Using a pair of 4-mm (US 6) needles and Clay, cast on 22 (24, 24, 28) sts. Work in garter st (see stitch guide) for 11 (15, 17, 23) rows or 2.5 [3, 4, 5] cm (1 [1¼, 1½, 2] in), ending on a WS row.

Eyelet row (RS): (k1, yo, k2tog) 3 times, k4 (6, 6, 10), (k2tog, yo, k1) 3 times.

FEET (MAKE TWO)

Row 1 (WS): K8 (8, 8, 9), p6 (8, 8, 10), k8 (8, 8, 9).
Row 2 (RS): Knit.
Rep rows 1 and 2, 10 (11, 12, 14) more times, then row 1 one more time.

TOES (MAKE TWO)

Row 1: K7 (7, 7, 8), k2tog tbl, k4 (6, 6, 8), k2tog, k7 (7, 7, 8). 20 (22, 22, 26) sts.
Row 2: K8 (8, 8, 9), p4 (6, 6, 8), k8 (8, 8, 9).
Row 3: K7 (7, 7, 8), k2tog tbl, k2 (4, 4, 6), k2tog, k7 (7, 7, 8). 18 (20, 20, 24) sts.
Row 4: K8 (8, 8, 9), p2 (4, 4, 6), k8 (8, 8, 9).

SIZES 0–3 MONTHS

Row 5: K7, k2tog tbl, k2tog, k7. 16 sts.
Row 6: Knit.
Row 7: *K2tog; rep from * to end. 8 sts.

SIZE 3–6 AND 6–9 MONTHS

Row 5: K7, k2tog tbl, k2, k2tog, k7. 18 sts.
Row 6: K8, p2, k8.
Row 7: K7, k2tog tbl, k2tog, k7. 16 sts.
Row 8: Knit.
Row 9: *K2tog; rep from * to end. 8 sts.

SIZE 9–12 MONTHS

Row 5: K8, k2tog tbl, k4, k2tog, k8. 22 sts.
Row 6: K9, p4, k9.
Row 7: K8, k2tog tbl, k2, k2tog, k8. 20 sts.
Row 8: K9, p2, k9.
Row 9: K8, k2tog tbl, k2tog, k8. 18 sts.
Row 10: Knit.
Row 11: *K2tog; rep from * to end. 9 sts.

FINISHING OFF

Break the yarn, leaving an 18 [20.5, 23, 25.5] cm (7 [8, 9, 10] in) tail. Using the tapestry needle, thread the tail through remaining sts, slip them off the needle and pull tight to secure. Use whip stitch to seam the booties closed, starting at the cast-off toe stitches and working up to the cuff. Carefully weave in the ends using a tapestry needle. Lace leather, ribbon or yarn through the eyelets for tying securely.

Pattern notes

- Tension: 22 sts and 30 rows to 10 cm (4 in) in stocking stitch on 4-mm (US 6) needles. Adjust the needle size if necessary to obtain the correct tension.

- Stitch guide: Garter stitch (worked over any number of sts) – knit every row.

Finished size

- From cuff to toe: 11.5 [12.5, 14, 16.5] cm (4½ [5, 5½, 6½] in)

- Circumference to fit 0–3 (3–6, 6–9, 9–12) months: 10 [11, 11.5, 12.5] cm (4 [4¼, 4½, 5] in)

- Booties shown fit 0–3 months

Knit 2 together through back loop (k2tog tbl)

- Insert the right needle into the back of the next two stitches on the left needle. The right needle is positioned behind the left.

- Pull the yarn through both stitches and drop them off the left needle.

Crochet baby blanket

This baby blanket pattern by Charlotte Rivers, from London, UK, is a good starting project for a beginner crocheter and equally good for an experienced crafter. This tutorial uses grey as a base colour, mixes it in with assorted brights, and finishes it with a simple edge. You could make this blanket with as many different colour yarns as you like, so it is a good way to use up odd balls of yarn.

MAKING THE BLANKET

To start: Ch6 with any colour B, join with a sl st to make a ring.

Round 1: Ch3, 2tr into the middle of the ring, ch3, (3tr into the middle of the ring, ch3) 3 times; join to the third chain of the beginning chain with a sl st.

Round 2: Using A, join yarn, ch3, 2tr into the same space (ch1, 3tr into the next space, ch3, 3tr into the same space) 3 times; ch1, 3tr into the starting corner, ch3; join to third chain of beginning chain with a sl st.

Round 3: Using any colour B, join yarn, ch3, 2tr into the same space; (ch1, 3tr into the next space; ch1, 3tr, ch3, 3tr into the corner space) 3 times; ch1, 3tr into the next space; ch1, 3dc into the starting corner, ch3; join to third chain of beginning chain with sl st.

Round 4: Using any colour B, join yarn, ch3, 2tr into the same space; (ch1, 3tr into the next space; ch1, 3tr into the next space; ch 1, 3tr, ch3, 3tr into the corner space) 3 times; ch1, 3tr into the next space; ch1, 3tr into the next space; ch1, 3tr into the starting corner, ch3; join to third chain of beginning chain with sl st.

Rounds 5–24: Continue working in rounds alternating the A and B colours as you choose. With every round, you will increase by one cluster on each side of the square.

EDGING THE BLANKET

Round 1: Using A, join yarn, create a final round of tr clusters around your blanket.

Round 2: Using the same colour, ch1, dc into top of ch2 from previous round, then dc into each stitch along this edge (99dc).
You are now at the first corner. 2dc into next stitch, 1dc into the next, 2dc into the next. You are now at the second edge. Dc into each stitch along the edge (99dc).
You are now at the second corner. 2dc into next stitch, 1dc into the next, 2dc into the next. You are now at the third edge. Dc into each stitch along the edge (99dc). You are now at the third corner.
2dc into next stitch, 1dc into the next, 2dc into the next. You are now at the fourth edge. Dc into each stitch along the edge (99dc). You are now at the fourth (and first) corner. 2dc into next stitch, 1dc into the next, 2dc into the next. Join to first dc with a sl st.

Rounds 3 and 4: As in round 2, dc along the edges of the blanket remembering to 2dc, 1dc, 2dc at each corner.

Fasten off and weave in ends. Lay work out flat and gently steam with an iron.

NOTE

If you are a beginner crocheter, you can find full details of the stitches used in the pattern on pages 134–7, and a list of abbreviations on page 138.

Pattern notes

Tension: 4 rounds = 10 cm (4 in) square

Finished size

70 cm (27½ in)

Inspiration gallery

Right: A crochet blanket is the perfect gift for a soon-to-be new mum. Delia Randall of Delia Creates made this very beautiful keepsake blanket using a basket-weave crochet stitch in simple cream yarn. She has edged it using double crochet in a suitably muted colour.

Below: For those with more than one child, a separate box will be required for each one. This painted monogram box by Wendy Harrison of Letterfest allows for a personal, but consistent, set.

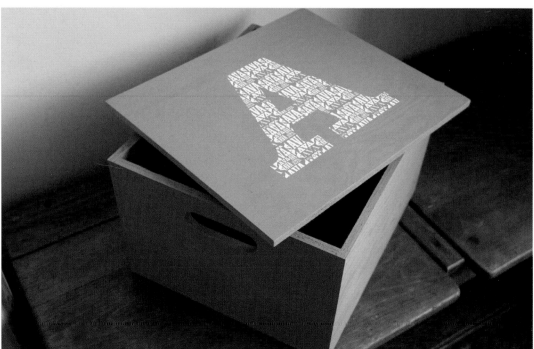

Above: Hand-knitted using 100% natural undyed lambswool, these socks were made by Dovile Mikelėnienė of Gera Bloga. The soft wool is perfect for newborn feet, since it allows the skin to breathe and prevents overheating.

Top right: This quilt uses distinctive and bold fabrics to create a fun, reversible design. Kelly Grooters of Petunias by Kelly followed the patterns of the material to create a quilted look while using only one piece of fabric for each side.

Right: This modern interpretation of a classic pixie bonnet by Kristi Morrow of SweetKM uses simple lines and a cosy fastening to show off baby's chubby cheeks perfectly.

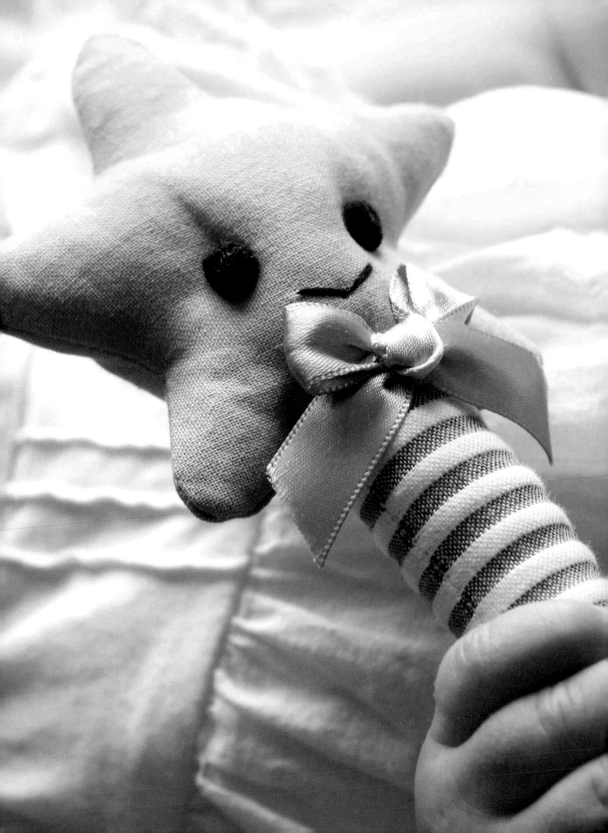

CHAPTER 3
WELCOMING THE BABY

Bunting birth announcement

Andrea Hanki is primarily a portrait and wedding photographer at Pink Sugar Photography based in Edmonton, Alberta, Canada, but she is also a crafter and mother to three young children. Here she shows us how to create a birth announcement that will be sure to make hearts melt. The stitched elements on the card add a splash of colour and texture to create a unique announcement. You could also frame one as a precious keepsake for the baby's room.

YOU WILL NEED

For 50 announcements:

- 50 photographs and 50 cards or 100 double-sided pre-printed birth announcements
- 51 cm (20 in) of fabric or four sheets of A4 card in a colour and pattern of your choice
- Scissors
- Glue stick
- Sewing machine (or hand-sewing needle and thread)

CRAFT TIME

- 2 hours

1. Print out 50 photographs of your little one and design, or write another card with birth statistics on it (name, date of birth, length, weight and so on.) When designing the text side of the card, be sure to leave the bottom half empty for sewing on the bunting.

2. Cut out four fabric or card triangles of equal sizes for each announcement. The triangles should be roughly 1.3 x 2 x 2 cm (½ x ¾ x ¾ in) for a 10 x 14 cm (4 x 5½-in) card or 1.3 x 6.5 x 6.5 cm (½ x 2½ x 2½ in) for a 12.5 x 18-cm (5 x 7-in) card.

3. Form a curved line by placing four triangles on to the information side of the card beneath the text. Glue the top edge of each triangle to the card.

4. Using a sewing machine, stitch the triangles to the card, making a curved line with the thread. You can also sew them on by hand with running stitch.

5. Glue the edges of a birth-statistics card and a photo card together and stitch around all four edges of the card. I find it looks best to sew with the photo side of the announcement facing up.

6. Trim any loose strings and your announcement is complete. Repeat the process for the rest of your cards.

Appliqué welcome banner

YOU WILL NEED

- Computer and printer
- A4 paper
- One or two pieces of 139.5-cm (55-in)-wide patterned fabric, measuring 20.5 x 51 cm (8 x 20 in)
- Scissors
- Iron and ironing board
- Hand-sewing needle and thread (or sewing machine)
- Interfacing 20.5 x 51 cm (8 x 20 in)
- Pins
- Plain linen fabric 45 x 55 cm (17¾ x 21¾ in)
- Simple printed fabric 45 x 59.5 cm (17¾ x 23½ in)
- Dowel or similar type of rod 50 cm (19¾ in) long x 1 cm (⅜ in) wide
- Ribbon 50 cm (19¾ in) long x 2.5–5 cm (1–2 in) wide

CRAFT TIME

- 2–3 hours

A welcome banner with the name of the new arrival is a great addition to any nursery and adds a sweet personal touch. This banner was created by Shannon Lamden of AuntyCookie, a freelance pattern designer, illustrator and crafter based in Melbourne, Australia. She produces homewares and artwork as well as fabrics. The patterned fabrics used to make the letters and shapes for this banner, Scallop Knit and Rulers, were designed by Lamden for RileyBlake fabrics.

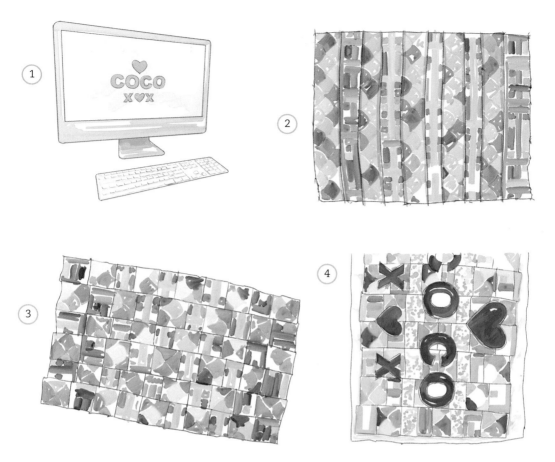

1. Use a computer to create the text and any shapes you would like on your banner. We advise using a simple typeface, which will be straightforward to cut and sew. If you have a talent for hand lettering or would like to use a serif or cursive font, then please do so; it will make the sewing more time consuming, but will look pretty. Enlarge your design to fill an A4-sized page.

2. For this project we have used two types of patterned fabric for the letters and sewn them together to create more interest and detail in the letters. You can use just one piece of patterned fabric if you prefer. If you choose to use two, patch them together to create one A4-sized piece of fabric. To do this, cut two strips of fabric into 10 x 25-cm (4 x 9¾-in) strips and then sew them together in stripes.

3. Press all seams flat, then cut vertical strips 10 cm (4 in) wide. Sew them together to create a grid. Iron all seams flat, cover the back with interfacing and iron again. The interfacing will create a stiffer block of fabric.

4. Cut out the letters and shapes from the paper. Pin each letter to the fabric and cut around it, being careful to follow the edges. If you want to you can skip the internal holes of the letters because these can be very fiddly.

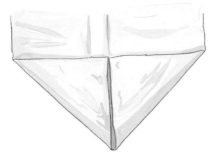

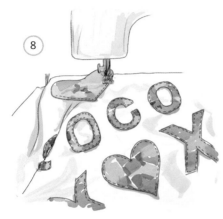

5. Take the plain linen fabric, which will form the front of the banner. To create the pointed flag bottom, fold the rectangle in half vertically so that you can see a faint crease through the centre of the fabric. Fold each bottom corner inwards to the crease and cut along the diagonal edges you have created.

6. Repeat for the simple printed piece, which will be the back of the banner.

7. Place the cut-out letters on the front piece of banner fabric. Work out a layout that you are happy with, remove the paper and then pin each letter to the fabric.

8. You are now ready to sew your letters to the banner. If you are sewing by hand, use a running stitch, or a straight stitch if you are using a sewing machine. The letters have raw edges and will fray slightly, giving the banner a rustic vibe. Trim any stray sewing threads and press flat with an iron.

9. Place the front and back pieces of the banner together with the text facing inwards and the right side of the printed fabric also facing inwards. Sew the sides and point of the banner together using a running stitch or straight stitch. Leave the top straight edge open across the entire width.

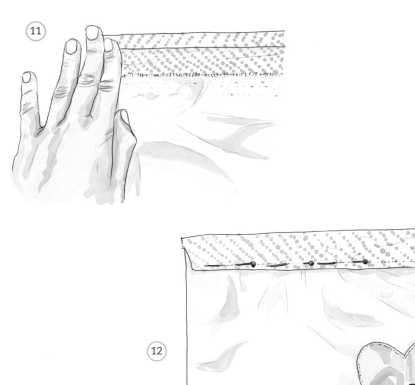

10. Turn the banner the right way out, making sure you poke out the points. Press it flat.

11. You should have about 5 cm (2 in) of excess printed or patterned backing fabric left at the top of the banner. Make a 10-cm (4-in) fold at the top to create a hem.

12. Fold over from the back to the front at the top edge of the fabric, leaving a 5-cm (2-in) gap for the dowel (or wood) to slip through. You will now have a strip of patterned fabric showing along the top of the front of the banner. Pin to the front of the banner ready to sew.

13. Sew along the pinned fold as close to the edge as you can, using running stitch or straight stitch.

14. Push your dowel (or wood) through the fold.

15. Tie the ribbon to each end of the dowel so you can hang your banner.

Star wand rattle

YOU WILL NEED

- Pencil
- Tracing paper
- Thin card
- Scissors
- 30 x 15 cm (12 x 6 in) cotton fabric for star
- Pins
- Hand-sewing needle and thread (or sewing machine)
- Chopstick or knitting needle
- Iron and ironing board
- Polyester fibrefill
- Small bell
- 30 x 15 cm (12 x 6 in) cotton fabric for wand
- Black embroidery thread
- Ribbon 15–20 cm (6–8 in) long by 1 cm (³⁄₈ in) for bow at neck

CRAFT TIME

- 1 hour

Lainie Wicks is the creative behind Maker*Land. Based in Perth, Western Australia, she likes to try her hand at a variety of crafts but particularly sewing, knitting, crochet and paper arts. She makes vintage-style clothing for her children as well as accessories and dressing-up outfits. Here she shows us how to create a star wand rattle that is ideal for little hands. This tutorial can be adapted so once you are confident making the star wand, you can experiment with different shapes or create other characters.

TEMPLATE

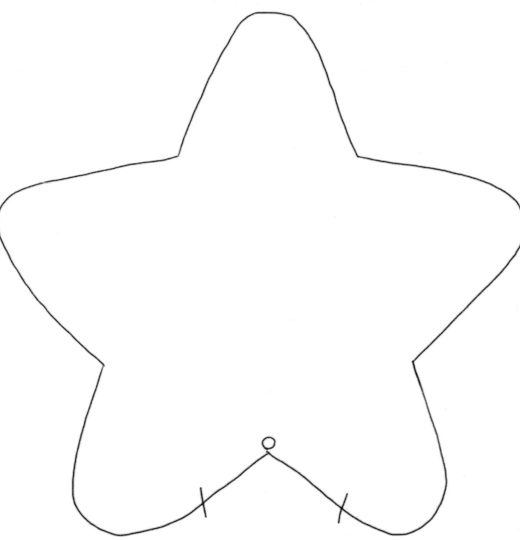

PREPARING THE PATTERNS

Reduce and trace the star template on to tracing paper
and then on to thin card. Cut it out. Be sure to mark the
opening for the wand at the bottom and a small 'O' point
(see Step 1). Make a pattern for your wand by cutting out
a piece of thin card measuring 3.8 x 19 cm (1½ x 7 ½ in).
Round off corners at each end.

Scaled up to 150% of actual size

1. Take the piece of fabric for the star and fold it in half widthways, right sides together. Place the star template on the fabric and trace around it in pencil on the uppermost side, ensuring you mark the opening.

2. Mark the 'O' point by passing a pin through both pieces of fabric then marking this point with a pencil on both the front and back. Sew along the pencil lines of the star shape using a straight stitch if sewing by machine, or a small, tight backstitch if hand-sewing. Remember to keep the points of the star rounded and do not sew the opening. Trim around the star shape 6 mm (¼ in) away from the stitching.

3. Mark the 'O' point with a few stitches through each individual layer of fabric. Clip into the corners of your star with scissors. Do not clip the opening area.

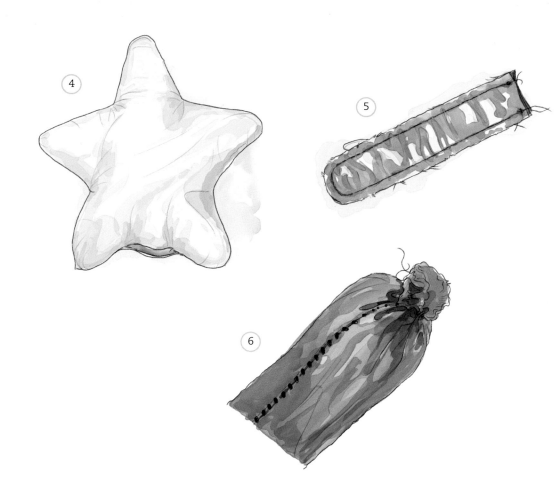

4. Turn the star the right way out and poke the corners through with a chopstick or knitting needle. Press with an iron and stuff through the opening. Wrap the bell in stuffing and place it in the middle of the star. Do not overstuff because you will need to insert the handle later on.

5. Fold the wand handle fabric lengthways. Pin the wand pattern piece to the fabric and cut two wand pieces. Place these right sides together and pin them. Using a small straight stitch or running stitch, sew along one long side, around the curved end and up the other side. Clip the curves at the rounded end.

6. Turn the wand right side out and stuff this part firmly. Sew along the top, gathering it together so it is firmly closed.

NOTES

- You can sew this project by hand or by machine.

- The wand does not have to have a face.

- You could use different print fabrics for the wand and the star.

- Disclaimer: Always supervise your baby when playing with toys. Even though this project is stitched very tight, some babies are experts at picking things apart!

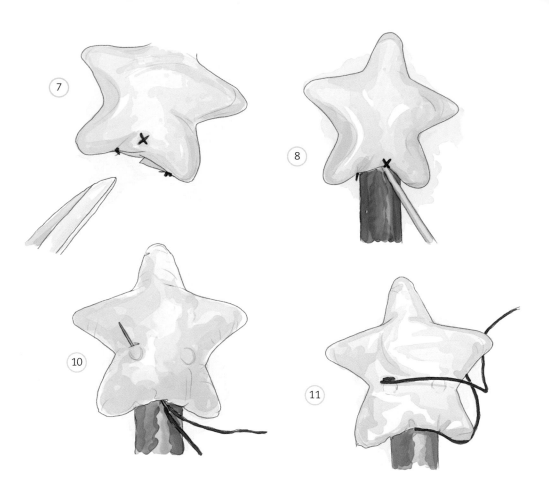

7. Use scissors to carefully snip into the bottom of the star, both front and back, from the edge towards the 'O' point. Clipping into this mark and shaping it into a point after you attach the handle to the star will give it a better shape.

8. Pull the star on to the wand. At the bottom, where you clipped up to the 'O' point, gently push the edges inwards until a neat inverted corner is formed. Use a knitting needle (or similar) to run along the edges, teasing them inside both front and back, and then pin into place.

9. With a needle and thread, sew the star to the wand with small, tight stitches. Go around twice to make sure the star is firmly attached.

10. You are now ready to sew the face. Mark the circular eye positions with pencil on the star. Thread a needle with embroidery thread, knotting the end to leave a tail of around 6.5 cm (2½ in). Enter the head through the base of the neck, bringing the needle out at the top of the left eye.

11. Working across the width of the eye, embroider with satin stitch: work straight stitches close together, increasing and decreasing in width to fit the small circles you marked out.

12. Once you have finished the left eye, push the needle into the head and bring it out at the top of the right eye. Complete in the same way.

13. Now push the needle back through the head, exiting through the neck. Cut the thread, leaving a tail of about 6.5 cm (2½ in). Tie the tails together and trim.

14. Embroider a mouth using three strands of embroidery thread. Insert the needle up through the neck, then bring it out at the left corner of mouth (A), before taking it across and inserting it at the right corner of the mouth (B). Bring it out at a point central to (A) and (B), but slightly lower (C). Insert the needle into the star over the horizontal long stitch and insert it directly underneath (D). Bring it out at the neck, oversew to secure and trim the threads.

15. Make a bow from the ribbon and attach it to the neck of the wand, sewing through at least seven or eight times to ensure it is really secure.

Hand-sewn cushion

An Kuppens is a Belgian designer who creates patterns and tutorials for her brand StraightGrain. She focuses on creating clothing for babies and girls as well as home decoration and bags. Here she shows us how to create a hand-sewn cushion that is ideal for a baby's nursery. You can also machine-sew this project. You can use any fabrics – mix and match to create a collection of cushions. The fabrics used here are Octoberama Blue and Red Eye Vireo, both by Charley Harper for Birch.

YOU WILL NEED

- Cushion
- Woven fabric (cotton, canvas or linen)
- Piping
- Iron-on transfer fabric
- Scissors
- Iron
- Hand-sewing needle and thread (or sewing machine)

CRAFT TIME

- 1.5 hours

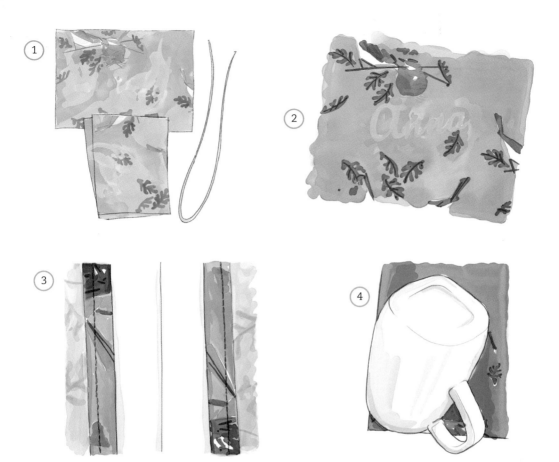

1. Measure the cushion and cut out the fabrics.
Front: width of cushion +2 cm (¾ in) x height of cushion + 2 cm (¾ in).
Back: two pieces of fabric. Both pieces: width of cushion ÷ 2 + 6 cm (2⅜ in) x height of cushion + 2 cm (¾ in).
Piping: circumference of cushion + 5 cm (2 in).
You will have three pieces of fabric and piping as shown.

2. Cut out the name using the iron-on transfer fabric. Either write it out or print it on a piece of paper first. Cut it out with scissors, pin it to transfer paper and cut around it. Take off the paper. Iron the name onto the front piece of fabric in the bottom right-hand corner.

3. Now hem the right edge of the left back piece, and the left edge of the right back piece. To do this, fold over 1 cm (⅜ in) of fabric (front side to back side) and press with an iron. Fold in again by another 1 cm (⅜ in) and press again. Stitch along both lengths near the edge using backstitch if sewing by hand, or straight stitch if using a sewing machine.

4. Round off the four non-hemmed corners of the front piece, and the two non-hemmed corners of the back pieces. A mug or glass can help you achieve good round corners. Mark with a pencil, then cut around with scissors.

(5)

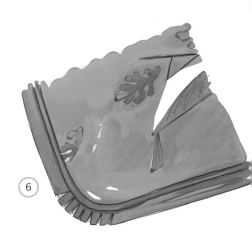

(6)

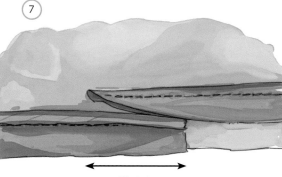

(7)

←——— 2 cm (¾ in) approx. ———→

(8)

5. Stitch the piping all around the edge of the front side of the front piece of fabric. Start by lining up the piping with the edge of the fabric at the centre of the bottom edge. Leave the first 1 cm (⅜ in) of the piping unstitched, then stitch close to the cording. If sewing by hand use backstitch; if using a sewing machine, use a zipper foot or a cording foot and straight stitch.

6. At the corners, clip the seam allowance of the piping.

7. When you are almost back at the beginning, cut off the end of the piping so you have an overlap of about 2 cm (¾ in).

8. Open up the end of the piping, exposing the cording. Cut the cording at the end of the piping so that it just meets the cording of the beginning.

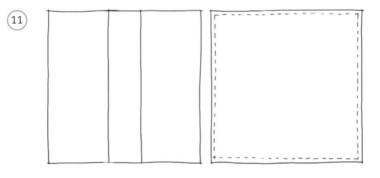

9. Fold in the casing of the piping end by 1 cm (³⁄₈ in), place it over the beginning of the piping, pin and then stitch near the cording.

10. Pin the back pieces of fabric on to the front piece, with right sides together. The hemmed edges of the back pieces should overlap each other by about 6 cm (2³⁄₈ in).

11. Turn the entire piece around so that the front piece is on top of the back pieces. You can now see the stitch lines that secure the piping onto the fabric (from Step 5). Stitch right into these stitches, all the way around the edge of the cushion cover, using backstitch if hand-sewing, and a zipper foot if using a machine. Cut away any excess fabric at the corners of the cusion cover.

12. Turn your cover the right way out and insert the cusion.

Felt animal book

Sanae Ishida is an illustrator and author living in Seattle, USA. She loves to make all manner of things but especially enjoys sewing clothes for her eight-year-old daughter and herself. Here she shows us how to create a hand-sewn felt baby book with animals – templates are on pages 78–9. This is a lovely little project that can be easily adapted; for instance, you could create a book with shapes, numbers or letters or even collections of fruit, vegetables or plants.

YOU WILL NEED

- 7 pieces of 18 x 18-cm (7 x 7-in) dark grey wool felt
- Scissors or rotary cutter and mat
- Wool felt in black, white, yellow, blue, brown and light grey – at least 15 x 15 cm (6 x 6 in) per colour
- Embroidery floss or regular thread (colours to match the felt pieces)
- Needle
- Ruler

CRAFT TIME

- 1 day

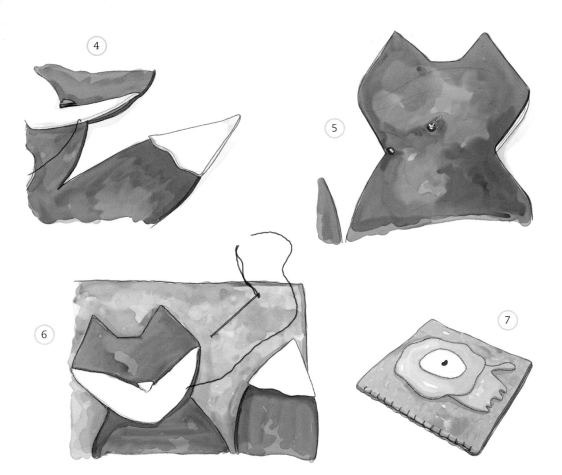

1. Using the templates on pages 78–9, enlarge and cut out the animal shapes, including all the parts.

2. Arrange the animal parts in the correct order to be stitched, as indicated on the templates. The numbers indicate the order in which they need to be sewn together.

3. Stitch the animal parts together, using a blind or running stitch, and colours that match the felt into which you are sewing. Always begin your first stitch from the underside of the fabric about 3 mm (⅛ in) from the edge.

4. Sew until you come to the end of a section, then pull the needle all the way through to the back of the fabric and knot it.

5. Once all your animals are assembled, you need to attach them to the pages. Start with the knotted end of the thread on the underside of the animal

6. Stitch on to the page using a blind or running stitch.

7. Use a blanket stitch to assemble the pages together.

TEMPLATES

Zebra

2

1

Elephant

1

Duck

1

Whale

1

Fox

Lion

Penguin

All scaled down to approx 40% of actual size

Inspiration gallery

CASPER
BEAR

BORN 1 MARCH
AT 10:25

TEN FINGERS

DUMMY

3.4 KG

61 CM

TEN TOES

Above: This arrival idea by Krystin McCourt of Sappy Apple makes a point of outlining all the specifics of the newborn. The addition of the measurements is a lovely way to show this information in a playful manner.

Left: Created by Josefine Degraa of Josefines Kinder, this name cusion is perfect for a new arrival. Featuring colourful contrasting letters, it should last for years to come.

Above left: These colourful toys have been handmade by Naomi Kimhi of Toela. Made with cotton fabric, they contain bells to make them rattle.

Above: This monogrammed embroidery hoop was created by Sam Owen of Minimanna using a hand-drawn letter template. The contrasting 'R' has been machine-stitched to the turquoise background and Owen then hand-embroidered the letter shadow with orange and pale pink embroidery floss.

Left: Photographing a baby directly against a decorative background is a great way of achieving an instant design without any need for technology or other skills. This is what Charlotte Rosenhoff did for the ornate and beautiful announcement of the arrival of her daughter Elvira.

CHAPTER 4
ONE MONTH OLD

Fabric blocks

Delia Randall is a sewist, crocheter, crafter and amateur photographer from Utah, USA. She blogs at Delia Creates about creating a handmade life that is both beautiful and practical. Here she shows us how to create a set of soft fabric blocks for baby. These blocks are great for little ones to play with from a young age and will grow well with them. Delia has created these blocks using fabrics from Cloud9, designed by Heather Moore of Skinny LaMinx. This tutorial shows you how to create one block, so repeat the instructions for the number of blocks you want to make.

1. Cut each fabric type to 12.5 x 23 cm (5 x 9 in). Cut a piece of interfacing for each piece of fabric in the same dimensions. You should have a total of three pieces of fabric and three pieces of interfacing.

2. Following the manufacturer's instructions, carefully iron the interfacing to each fabric piece.

3. Cut each fused piece of fabric down to two 10 x 10-cm (4 x 4-in) squares. To do this, use a ruler and washable fabric marker and draw the squares out on the interfacing side before cutting.

4. You should now have six fused-fabric squares measuring 10 x 10 cm (4 x 4 in), two in each fabric type.

5. Lay the fabric squares out as the illustration above shows. This will help you keep your fabric squares organised while you sew, so they will alternate evenly in the finished blocks.

6. Flip the bottom square on top of the square above it with right sides facing each other. You will be sewing the bottom edges together, but for ease of sewing, turn that edge up so it is at the top while you work. You may want to pin the pieces together so they do not shift while you sew.

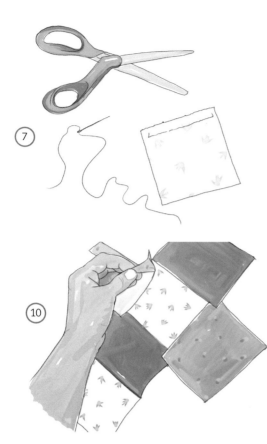

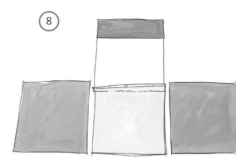

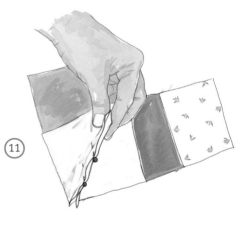

7. Thread the needle and knot the thread at one end. Starting 1.3 cm (½ in) below the edge and 1.3 cm (½ in) from the right side, sew all the way along the edge using a backstitch, stopping 1.3cm before the edge. When you get to the end of the line, backstitch into the last stitch twice, create a double knot and cut off the tail. If you are using a sewing machine, machine-sew the lines using a straight stitch, with a 1.3 cm (½ in) seam allowance. Remember to start and stop 1.3 cm (½ in) from the sides.

8. Take the sewn piece and lay it on top of the next piece above in your layout.

9. Continue sewing all the pieces in the middle of the layout together.

10. Sew the side pieces to the upper middle piece, being sure to leave 1.3-cm (½-in) gaps at the sides.

11. Pin the top and side edges together and sew them.

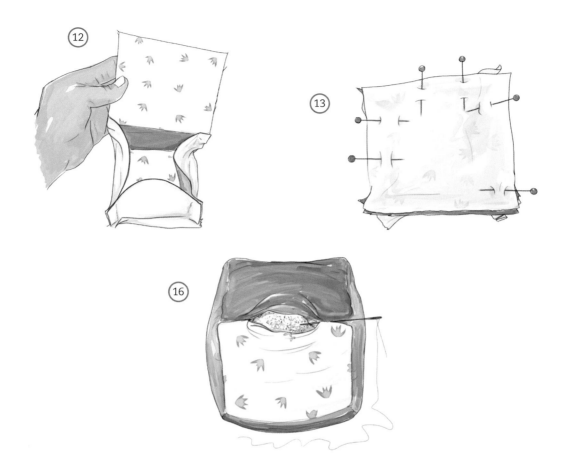

12. Continue sewing all of the edges together until you have one square left with only one edge sewn.

13. Pin the edges of the last square to the rest of the cube, completing the box.

14. Sew all the way around, leaving a 5-cm (2-in) opening on one of the edges.

15. Turn the cube right side out, through the opening. Use a chopstick, knitting needle or similar to push out the corners. Fill the cube with polyester fibrefill. Do not understuff, as the cube will not hold its shape, but also avoid over stuffing as the cube will become distorted.

16. Prep the opening by folding the seam allowance down with your fingers. Hand-sew the opening closed with a ladder stitch.

NOTE

Sew 1.3 cm (½ in) from all the sides to allow the corners to match up.

17. Once you have sewn up the opening and reached the other side, pull the stitches tight. Sew again in the other direction so the seam is secure and will not come undone. Cut the thread tail.

Crochet teether

This crochet teether by Charlotte Rivers based in London, UK is the perfect project for both beginner and experienced crafters. Here raw, untreated wooden beads and organic wool was used to make this teether and kept the yarn colours muted. You could also use different colours; this is a good way to use up odd balls or ends of yarn.

NOTE

If you are a beginner crocheter, you can find full details of the stitches used in the pattern on pages 134–7, and a list of abbreviations on page 138.

YOU WILL NEED

- 3 different colours of DK yarn, 1 for each crochet ball
- 3.25-mm (D/3) crochet hook
- Stitch marker
- 11 x 2.5-cm (1-in) round raw wooden beads, with hole
- Yarn needle
- Scissors

CRAFT TIME

- 1–2 hours

TEETHER

Make a sl st on your hook. Leave a 10-cm (4-in) tail. Work in rounds.

Round 1: Ch2, 6dc in 2nd chain from hook. 6 st.

Round 2: (2dc into each st) 6 times. 12 st.

Round 3: (1dc into first st, 2dc into next) 6 times. 18 st.

Rounds 4–5: Dc into each st around. 18 st.

Round 6: (Dc, dc2tog) 6 times (12). Make dc, insert the stitch marker into this stitch and complete the round.

ADD WOODEN BALL
Place a wooden ball into the cup shape, positioning the hole from top to bottom.

Round 7: (Dc, dc2tog) 4 times. 8 sts.
Remove stitch marker, make dc, insert stitch marker into this stitch and complete the round.

Round 8: (Dc, dc2tog) 2 times, 2dc. 6 sts. Remove stitch marker.

NOTE

Babies should only be allowed to play with this teether toy under supervision. Always check that all parts are secure before allowing a baby to play with it.

FINISHING OFF

Fasten off. Cut yarn, leaving a 10-cm (4-in) tail. Weave in ends securely by weaving around the holes at either end and then back over the stitches. Cut off excess yarn.

Repeat this on five of the eleven wooden balls using two of the same colour yarns twice and the other colour once.

JOINING AND FASTENING THE BEADS
Start by creating a small crochet ball. Make a sl st on your hook. Leave a 10-cm (4-in) tail.

Work in rounds.
Round 1: Ch2, 6dc in 2nd chain from hook. 6 st.

Round 2: (Dc, dc2tog) 2 times. 4 st.

Round 3: Dc, dc2tog, dc. 3st. Ch 45 in the same colour yarn. Fasten off. Cut yarn, leaving 20.5 cm (8 in) excess. Thread excess yarn through yarn needle. Thread the beads on to chain in this order: two raw wood beads; colour 1 bead (the same colour as the yarn you are threading on to); raw bead; colour 2 bead; raw bead; colour 3 bead; raw bead; colour 2 bead; raw bead; colour 1 bead.

Thread the needle and yarn back through the two first raw beads. Pull tight. Remove the yarn needle and undo any chain stitches that are visible until you are as close to the first raw bead as possible. Fasten off. Trim excess yarn so you have 10 cm (4 in) remaining. Rethread needle and weave this last end into the small ball you created at the beginning of the chain. Ensure you weave it in very securely. Go back and forth, in and out, and around the small ball many times, crossing through the centre a number of times until you feel it is fully secure. Cut off any excess yarn.

Double crochet 2 together (dc2tog)

- Insert the hook into the next stitch, catch the yarn and take it over the hook.

- Pull the yarn through. You should have two loops on your hook.

- Keeping the loops on the hook, insert the hook into the next stitch, catch the yarn and take it over the hook (yo).

- Pull it through. You should now have three loops on your hook.

- Catch the yarn, take it over the hook (yo) and pull through all three loops.

Stars and clouds paper mobile

YOU WILL NEED

- Wooden embroidery hoop, diameter 25.5 cm (10 in)
- Thin cotton yarn
- Scissors
- Masking tape
- Tracing paper
- Thin card at least 21.5 x 28 cm (8.5 x 11 in)
- Silver glitter paper
- Silver metallic paper
- White card in either matt or shiny
- Craft knife
- Cutting mat
- Metal ruler
- Tiny hole punch
- Glue stick
- Ceiling hook

CRAFT TIME

- 1–2 hours

Minhee Cho is a graphic designer and owner of Paper + Cup Design in New York, USA. Here she shows us how to create a paper stars and clouds mobile. This simple method offers endless opportunities for you to adapt and change the colour, materials or shapes to customise the mobile as you like. As well as using the templates provided here, you can also find ready-made hand punches in craft shops that are good for projects like these.

All scaled down to 75% of actual size

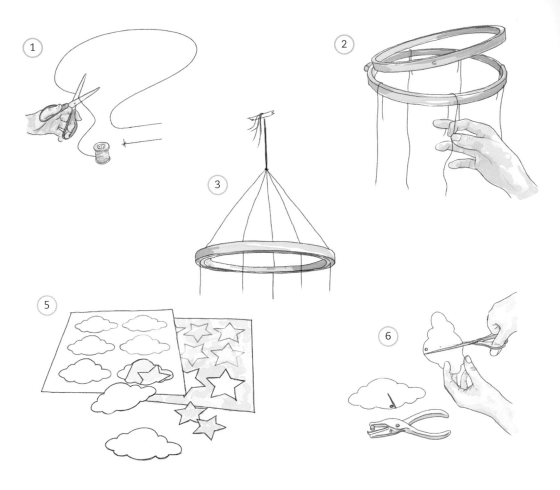

1. Prepare the hoop. We have used five strands for this mobile but you could use more if you want to make it fuller, or fewer if you would like it more minimal. Cut the yarn into lengths 122 cm (48 in) long.

2. Open up the hoop and place the pieces of cut yarn evenly around the circle. Half of the length of each piece of yarn should come out of the top of the hoop to provide the hanging length. Close up the hoop and tighten it (you can adjust the positions later it you need to).

3. Gather the top ends of the yarn and tie them together in a loose knot in the middle. Tape up the mobile and hang it up while you work. This will make it easier to position the items.

4. Enlarge and prepare the shapes. We have used 11 big stars, 13 small stars and 7 clouds. As the stars are two-sided and the clouds 3D you will need a total of 22 big star shapes, 26 small star shapes and 14 cloud shapes. Trace the star and cloud templates using tracing paper, transfer them on to card and cut them out with scissors.

5. Draw around the templates on the glitter paper and metallic paper for the stars (11 big on glitter, 13 small on glitter, 11 big on metallic, 13 small on metallic). Then draw 14 cloud shapes on white card.

6. Cut halfway through each cloud with the knife on the cutting mat, or scissors, measuring with the ruler. Cut half of them from the bottom up and the other half from the top down. Punch a hole in each. If the cut is from bottom, punch the top half; if it is from the top, punch the bottom half.

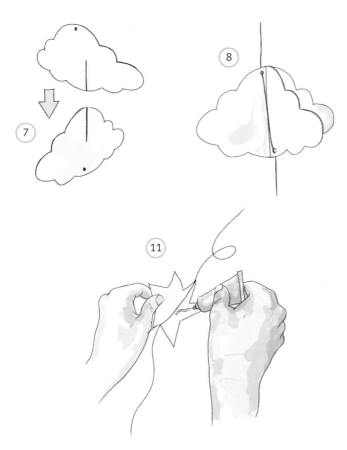

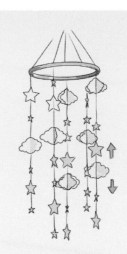

NOTE

You can adjust the position of the clouds at any time. If you are unsure about the positioning, add them all and finalise the positions by eye, before adding your stars.

7. Slot the opposing two pieces of each cloud together so that they become 3D.

8. Thread the clouds onto the yarn. On strand 1, thread the yarn through the two holes and pull the cloud to the top so it is about 7.5 cm (3 in) from the hoop.

9. Add the next cloud to strand 1, leaving a 3.8-cm (1½-in) gap where the star will go.

10. Repeat Steps 8 and 9 for the next strand, but alternate the positions so your clouds are at different levels to the neighbouring strand. Continue until you have filled all five strands.

11. Glue the stars into the gaps. Begin by putting glue on to one side of the star and placing it on the string with your finger. Gently tap to make it stick. Take the other star piece and press it to the first one, covering up the string to create a double-sided star.

12. Repeat Step 11 until all your stars are in place. Attach the ceiling hook and fix your mobile to it.

Painted baby grows (onesies)

Painting or printing a baby grow (onesie) is a really quick and easy way to create a personalised gift for a little one. You can make the design as simple or as complicated as you like – why not make several at the same time? This geometric version was created by Kristen Bach at TREEHOUSE kid & craft, from Athens, Georgia, USA. She runs a children's shop that specialises in modern and craft-based toys as well as running craft classes for babies all the way through to adults. Once you are confident with the tutorial, you could create your own designs and colour combinations.

YOU WILL NEED

- White baby grow
- Masking tape
- Small, flat paintbrush
- Paper plate or palette for mixing colours
- Acrylic paint
- Textile medium
- Iron and ironing board
- Pressing cloth (scrap of cotton fabric)

CRAFT TIME

- 1 hour

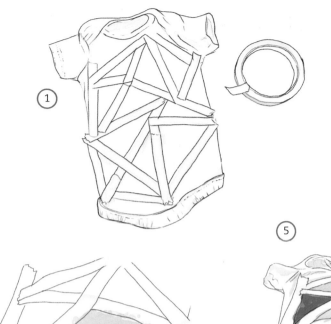

1. Tape off your design with masking tape. You can either follow the mosaic pattern used here, or create your own pattern.

2. Choose your colours and mix your paints. We chose a few different colours for our designs but you could go with two colours or even just one.

3. To prepare the paint you will need to add two parts textile medium to one part paint. The textile medium enables the colour to adhere to the fabric.

4. Paint inside the taped areas, then leave the baby grow to dry.

5. Once the paint is completely dry (after about 30 minutes), peel off the masking tape.

6. Place the pressing cloth over the baby grown and iron to heat-set the paint.

Inspiration gallery

Above: Creating a teether that can double as jewellery is a convenient and fashionable alternative to travelling with bulky toys. Jana of Nihama has designed a teething toy that the wearer will never lose and can wear with pride.

Left: Even a single crocheted wooden ring makes for a great teether. These teething rings by Aimee of Apple n Amos are simple but effective. The crocheted handles are made from cotton yarn and make the perfect handle for small fingers.

Above: The same principles for painting on onesies can be applied to other clothing items too. This bib by Amy Warkentin of Down Home Amy is screenprinted using water-based ink onto organic hemp/cotton fabric.

Left: Delia Randall created this black paper crane mobile for her daughters' room. She wanted something whimsical, yet bold and modern. It is made up of black paper cranes tied to the inner ring of a large embroidery hoop with black thread.

CHAPTER 5
FIRST BIRTHDAY

First-birthday crown

Lainie Wicks is the creative behind Maker*Land, based in Perth, Western Australia. Here she shows us how to make a cute first-birthday crown. Beyond a first-birthday party, this crown makes a great dress-up accessory. To make it fit an older toddler, all you need to do is unpick the elastic and replace it with a longer piece. Feel free to add your own decorating ideas for the crown, such as sequins or ribbons.

YOU WILL NEED

- A4 paper
- Pencil
- Scissors
- Thin card
- 35.5 x 20.5 cm (14 x 8 in) of printed cotton fabric for crown front
- 2 pieces of 35.5 x 20.5-cm (14 x 8-in) plain cotton fabric for crown backing
- 35.5 x 20.5 cm (14 x 8 in) of wadding
- Pins
- Hand-sewing needle and strong thread (or sewing machine)
- Chopstick or knitting needle
- Thin card or plastic, or a sheet of craft foam to use for stabilising the crown (plastic or foam will be easier to clean)
- 35.5 x 4.75-cm (14 x 1$\frac{7}{8}$-in) piece of printed or plain fabric for bottom binding
- 50-g (2-oz) skein of acrylic yarn for making pompoms
- Fork
- 20.5 cm (8 in) length of elastic, 2 cm (¾ in) wide
- Optional: beads, ribbon and sequins for extra decoration

CRAFT TIME

- 2 hours (hand-sewn) or 1 hour (machine-sewn)

TEMPLATE

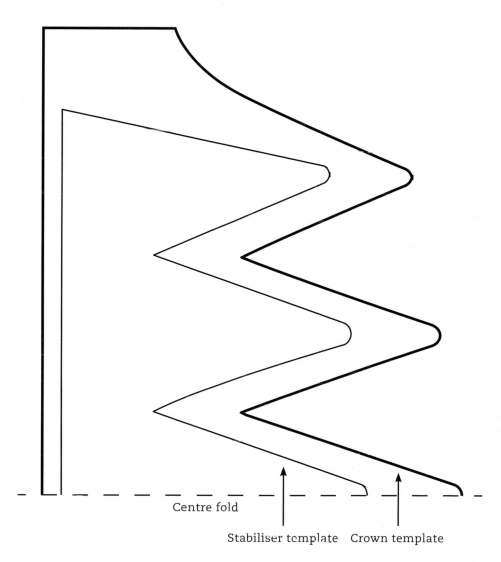

Centre fold

Stabiliser template   Crown template

Scaled down to 85% of actual size

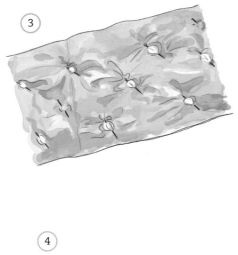

TIP

When sewing the angles at the base of the points, sew down to the base, stop and sew one single stitch across before sewing back up towards the point. This helps to avoid puckering.

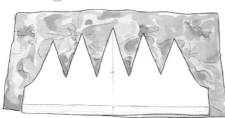

1. Enlarge and prepare your templates. Fold a sheet of A4 paper in half widthways and press in the crease. Unfold and, placing the crease on the centre fold line of the pattern template, trace the half crown shape. Refold the paper and cut out the shape. Unfold and glue the paper on to card. When dry, cut out the template. Now make the template for the stabiliser in the same way.

2. Prepare the fabric and wadding. Place the crown backing fabric face up on a flat surface. Place the crown front fabric face down on top of it, right sides together. Place the wadding on top of the two pieces of fabrics and the other piece of plain cotton backing fabric on top of the wadding. This top piece of cotton allows all the layers to be sewn together more easily. It will also provide a good surface for drawing around your template.

3. Pin all the layers together, keeping the surfaces as smooth as possible.

4. Place the crown template on the pinned layers, with the bottom edge of the template positioned along the bottom edge of the fabric layers. Trace around the template with a pencil.

5. Sew along the pencil lines, making sure you keep the points of the crown slightly rounded. If sewing by hand use a small backstitch; if sewing on a machine, use straight stitch.

6. Trim around the crown shape, around 3 mm (⅛ in) from the stitching.

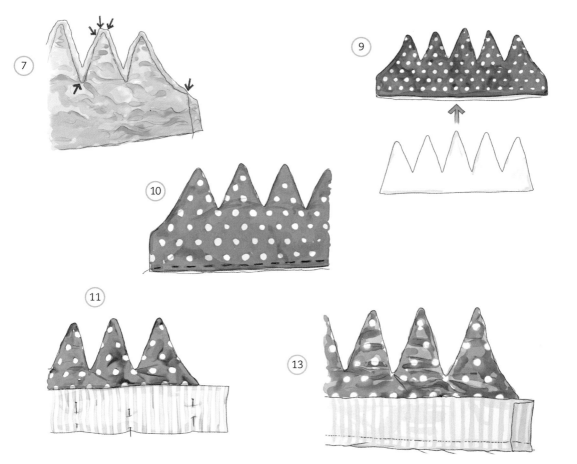

7. Carefully clip around the upper points, and into the base angles. Clip the corners at the edges. Carefully clip the wadding and plain cotton from around the stitching too, to help with turning.

8. Turn the crown inside out so that the outer and inner crown fabrics are on the outside. Use the end of a pencil to help to turn out the crown points completely. Press with an iron.

9. Trace the stabiliser template on to the foam, plastic sheet or card. Cut out the shape and slip it into the crown between the wadding and the plain fabric, sliding the stabilizer's points into the crown's points.

10. Baste the bottom edges of the crown together. This will help keep the layers in place when you attach your binding.

11. Pin the binding strip of fabric along the bottom edge of the crown, right sides together, leaving about 6 mm (¼ in) extending over the edge.

12. Turn in the overhanging short ends so they are in line with the edges, and pin.

13. Sew along the bottom edge with a 6-mm (¼-in) seam allowance.

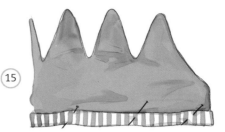

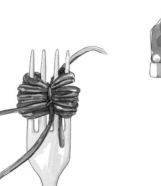

14. Fold the binding strip away from the crown and press. Turn the crown over. Fold in the raw edge of the binding to meet the edge of the crown, and press again.

15. Fold the binding again on to the back of crown, so it encloses the bottom edge and forms a neat strip. Pin and hand baste the strip into place.

16. Turn over to the right side and stitch in the 'ditch' between the crown and the binding. Use a small backstitch if sewing by hand, or straight stitch if using a machine.

17. Next, make the pompoms. Wrap the yarn around the outside of a dinner fork about 50 times and then cut the end of the yarn. Cut a piece of yarn about 20.5 cm (8 in) long and tie it tightly around the wraps between the fork's centre prongs, using a double knot.

18. Slip the yarn off the fork and cut the loops at the edges. Gently roll the pompom between your hands to fluff. You will trim it later once it is in place on the crown. Repeat four times.

NOTE

The binding at the back should look neatly topstitched. Remember to remove your basting stitches.

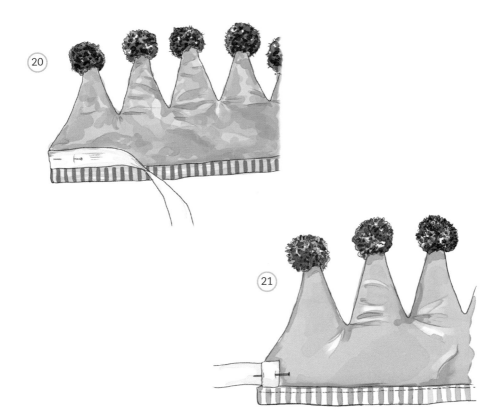

19. With a needle and double thread, securely stitch one pompom to each point on your crown. Once all five are stitched on, trim with scissors so they are neat and all a similar size.

20. Place the elastic at the back of the crown as shown. Stitch in place 2 cm (¾ in) from the edge.

21. Fold the elastic over itself and stitch again, close to the edge of the crown and around the edge of the square shape, so that it is really secure.

22. To be sure of size, check the fit on your little one's head before cutting the elastic and sewing it onto the other end. It should be firm but not too tight. You can further decorate the crown with sequins, bows or more pompoms if you wish.

NOTE

The elastic should look like this from the front.

Ruffle party skirt

Crystal Motes from Florida, USA loves to sew, craft, create DIY projects and blog about them at Stitched by Crystal. Here she shows us how to make a super-cute ruffle party skirt, which is ideal for a first-birthday party, or everyday wear. For this tutorial Crystal has used Liberty of London Classic Tana Lawn fabric in Wild Flowers Mauve, Cream and Pink. The finished skirt measures 23 cm (9 in) long, which will fit an average one-year-old. To make the skirt to a specific size, see page 109.

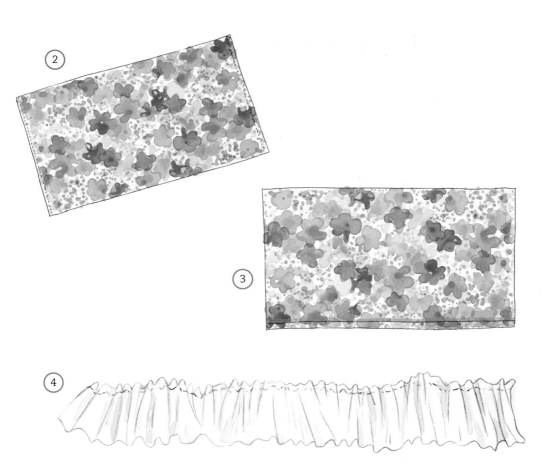

1. Wash and dry the fabrics before starting work. Measure out and cut them as follows: top tier 2 x pieces 12.5 x 45.5 cm (5 x 18 in); middle tier 2 x pieces 19 x 45.5 cm (7½ x 18 in); bottom tier 2 x pieces 25.5 x 45.5 cm (10 x 18 in). Cut the tulle into four strips, each measuring 11.5 x 114.5 cm (4.5 x 45 in).

2. Put the two bottom-tier pieces right sides together, pin them along the short sides and sew with a 1-cm (⅜-in) seam allowance. Use running stitch if sewing by hand, and straight stitch if using a machine.

To prevent fraying, finish the seams with blanket or whip stitch if sewing by hand, zigzag stitch on a machine, or an overlocker. Press the seams with an iron.

3. Hem the bottom of this tier by ironing the bottom edge under 1 cm (⅜ in), then under another 1 cm (⅜ in) and sewing along the folded edge. Use running stitch or straight stitch. Repeat Steps 2 and 3 with the middle and top tiers.

4. Fold one of the tulle strips in half, lining up the long edges. Gather the strip along

the folded edge by sewing a basting stitch 1 cm (⅜ in) from the folded edge, then pulling on the bottom thread to gather the fabric until it is about 45.5 cm (18 in) long. Repeat with all of the tulle strips.

5. With a tailor's pencil or water-soluble marker, draw a line around the bottom and middle tiers 7.5 cm (3 in) above the hem.

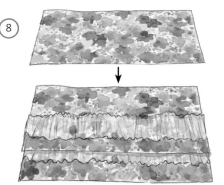

6. Pin one of the tulle ruffles along the line you drew across the front of the bottom tier. Pin a second tulle ruffle along the line you drew across the back of the tier. The ruffles should overlap slightly at the side seams.

7. Use running stitch if sewing by hand and straight stitch if using a machine. Sew over the basting stitch, 1 cm (⅜ in) from the folded edge. Repeat Steps 6 and 7 to attach the remaining two ruffles on the middle tier.

8. With all three tiers right side out, tuck the bottom tier inside the middle tier and line up the raw edges. Then tuck the top tier inside the other tiers, and line up the raw edges of all three tiers.

9. You should have the bottom tier sandwiched between the top and middle tiers. You will flip this the right way out later.

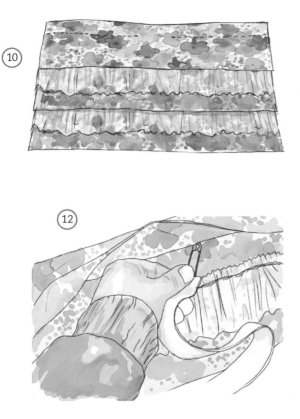

(10)

(12)

Adapting the ruffle skirt

For a more casual skirt, the tulle ruffles can be left off.

You can also modify this skirt to make any size. Determine the length of the skirt by measuring from the waist to the knee of the wearer. For the width, measure around the waist. Cut the bottom tier pieces 3.2 cm (1¼ in) longer than the length measurement and 2.5 cm (1 in) wider than the waist measurement. The middle and top tiers will be the same width as the bottom tier but will be 6.5 cm and 12.5 cm (2½ in and 5 in) shorter respectively. For an older child, you may choose to cut the middle and top tiers even shorter so they are more proportionate to the size of the child. Cut the elastic to the same length as the waist measurement.

10. Pin the top raw edges of all three tiers together and then sew all the way around the top edge with a 1-cm (⅜-in) seam allowance. Use running stitch or straight stitch. You can now flip the top tier outside the skirt and iron the seam at the top.

11. Create a casing for the elastic by sewing around the skirt 3.2 cm (1¼ in) from the top edge. Start sewing towards the back of the skirt and stop sewing when you are about 5 cm (2 in) from your starting point. Use running stitch or straight stitch.

12. Attach a safety pin to the end of the elastic to help feed it through the casing. Lift the top tier of the skirt and insert the elastic in the opening at the back of the skirt. Push elastic all the way through the casing until it comes out the other side.

13. Overlap the ends of the elastic about 2.5 cm (1 in) and sew them together using running stitch if sewing by hand, or a wide zigzag stitch on a machine. Stretch the waistband to pull all the elastic into the casing. Sew the hole closed using running stitch or straight stitch.

Harem pants

YOU WILL NEED

- Pattern: follow the QR code or weblink below to download it
- Pre-washed fabric, such as cotton, 110 x 50 cm (43¼ x 19¾ in)
- Pins
- Scissors
- Hand-sewing needle and thread (or sewing machine)
- Iron and ironing board
- Elastic 50 cm (19¾ in) long and about 2–3 cm (1 in) wide
- Medium-sized safety pin
- Tailor's chalk

CRAFT TIME

- 1 hour

Sweet Meadowsweet is run by Sarmite Strautina and Dace Seglina-Grinblate. Based in Riga, Latvia, they specialise in knitting and sewing clothes and accessories, mostly for children. This tutorial for their harem pants is a great project for a beginner sewer, and they can be made either by hand or on a machine. The pattern can easily be scaled up to make different sizes.

Size

This tutorial shows how to make the pants for a baby aged 12 to 18 months, but you can always adjust them slightly if you want to make them bigger or smaller.

Download the pattern here:
http://bit.ly/1mPDQx2

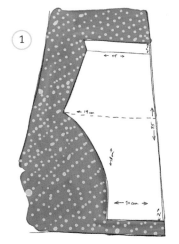

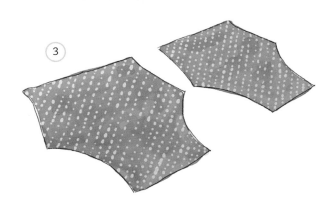

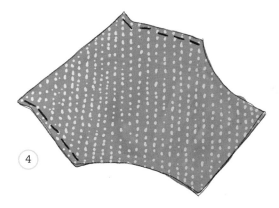

1. Fold the fabric in half vertically with the print facing outwards. Check that the fabric is positioned correctly, that any lines or characters on the print are straight, and that the fabric is vertical. Place the pattern on the fabric with the straight side as close as possible to the folded edge of the folded fabric.

2. Pin the pattern to the fabric. Draw around it with tailor's chalk. Cut around the pattern, leaving a 1-cm (⅜-in) seam allowance. Lines on the illustration for Step 1 indicate where you need to cut.

3. Repeat Step 2 so that you have two pieces of cut fabric. The illustration shows how they will look unfolded.

4. Lay the two pieces of fabric on top of one another, right sides together. Sew the two top seams together, as indicated, leaving a 1-cm (⅜-in) seam allowance. Use backstitch if sewing by hand, and straight stitch if using a machine. To neaten up the seam, you can use whip stitch (if sewing by hand) or zigzag stitch (on a machine).

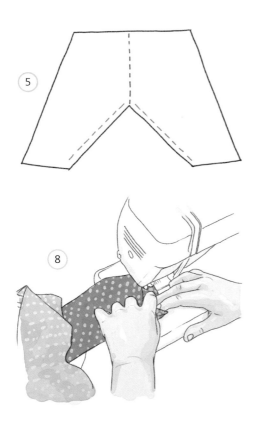

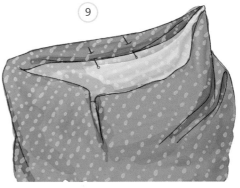

5. Unfold the fabric so the seams you have stitched are at the centre (back and front) as illustrated in red. The next seam you are going to sew is shown in grey.

6. Pin the fabrics together to secure them. Sew the seam using backstitch or straight stitch. To neaten up the seam, you can use whip stitch or zigzag stitch. Press the seams you have just sewn.

7. With the pants still inside out, fold up the hems by 1 cm (⅜ in). Fold up the hem by another 1 cm (⅜ in). Pin into place.

8. Turn the pants the right way out and sew along the top of the folded hem seams, as close to the top of the fold as possible. Use backstitch or straight stitch.

9. Fold down the waist by 6 mm (¼ in), and fix with pins. Fold again by 2.5 cm (1 in), removing and reaffixing the pins as you go.

10. Sew along the lower edge along the whole waist, using backstitch or straight stitch.

11. Stop about 2.5 cm (1 in) from the end.

12. Fold the end of the elastic by 2.5 cm (1 in) and attach a safety pin.

13. Insert the pin in the opening and pull through the waist tunnel until it comes out the end.

14. Put both elastic ends together and sew them together.

15. Sew the opening together so that the elastic is secure inside the waistband, using backstitch or straight stitch.

Hand-stamped leggings

Zeena Shah is the designer and printmaker behind London-based Heart Zeena. She makes beautiful handprinted textiles and homewares from her East London studio. Here she shows us how to lino-print a pair of baby leggings using a number of her trademark characters, including an owl, a fox and a bird.

Scaled up to 130% of actual size

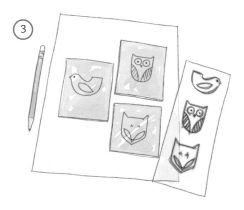

1. Print out the templates to scale on to A4 white paper. Using tracing paper, trace around each shape, making sure to add in all the details on the templates.

2. Flip over the tracing paper and transfer trace the drawings on to the lino blocks by re-drawing on top of your pencil line.

3. When you lift up the tracing paper, your pencil outlines will remain on the lino blocks.

4. Use scissors to trim any excess areas of lino away; this will save time later and avoid wasting time cutting out insignificant areas of lino.

5. Using a lino cutter, carefully gouge away all the areas on your design that you do not want to print, starting with the areas outside the pencil line. This is a very gradual process; start shallow and go deeper and deeper. Keep your fingers away from the blade at all times, and hold onto the lino

block as you cut. You will start to see the print area stand out. With a finer cutter tip, cut away the detailed areas of the design within the stamp shape. Stop cutting when you are happy with your lino stamp shape.

⑥

⑧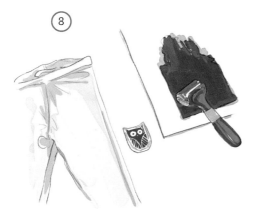

⑨

6. Repeat this process for all three stamps. Check again for excess lino and cut it away with scissors to neaten your shapes.

7. Press the black ink pad on to the stamps and test them out on plain paper. This will give you an accurate indication of the print. You may need to cut away further areas of lino. Keep testing your stamps until you are happy with the finished print. Mark on the leggings where you would like your prints to appear and check your design before you start printing.

8. Choose a stamp and squirt some fabric paint onto the inking tray; just a little will go a long way. Roll it out using the brayer until you have a very fine layer on your tray. Roll this ink on to your stamp, flip over the stamp carefully and place it on the leggings exactly where you want the stamp to appear. You will not be able to move it once you have put it face down.

9. Using a clean brayer, gently roll over the stamp to apply even pressure to your print. Lift away the stamp to reveal your print. Continue this process to create your desired design.

10. Repeat the process for each of your other stamps until you have beautifully printed leggings. Leave to dry overnight and iron on the reverse to heat set the fabric paint. The leggings will then be machine washable.

Circus-themed wooden blocks

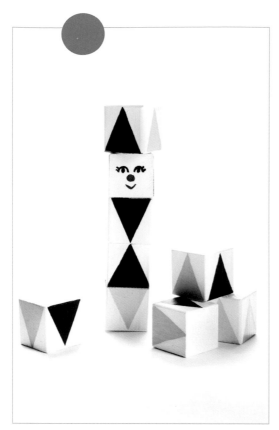

⭐

YOU WILL NEED

- Nine untreated wooden blocks, 4.5 cm (1¾ in) square (buy online from Etsy or from a local craft supplier)
- Acrylic paint in white, black, yellow, pink and turquoise
- Two paintbrushes (small for triangles, bigger for surface painting)
- Narrow masking tape
- Red and black pens suitable for wood
- Optional: clear varnish

CRAFT TIME

- 2–3 hours

Jenni Juurinen is an interior stylist and production designer based in Helsinki, Finland. She creates sets for films and TV, as well as working as a style editor for *Deko* magazine. Here she shows us how to create some circus-themed wooden stacking blocks, which make an ideal present for a one-year-old.

TEMPLATE

Scaled up to 130% actual size

118

1. Paint all the sides of the blocks with white paint and allow them to dry.

2. Use masking tape to make a triangle on one side of the block by arranging two pieces of masking tape from the top corners down, so that they come together at the lower edge of the block.

3. Paint the area inside the tapes with your chosen colour using a small paintbrush.

4. Remove the masking tape and leave to dry. It is best to remove the masking tape soon after painting, otherwise it might get stuck and leave uneven edges.

5. Paint a triangle in the same colour on all of the blocks.

6. Once the paint is dry, move on to your next colour and repeat Steps 2 to 5. Paint five sides of your blocks, leaving one side plain white.

7. Draw faces on the white side of each block using the template and the red and black pens.

8. To make the blocks more durable, you can treat all sides with clear varnish once the paint is dry.

Teeny tiny knitted mittens

★

YOU WILL NEED

· 6-ply soft sock yarn,
  1 skein of each colour:
  main colour (A),
  contrast colour (B),
  contrast colour (C)
· 1 pair of 2.25-mm
  (US 1) double-pointed
  knitting needles
· Stitch marker
· 1 pair of 3.25-mm
  (US 3) double-pointed
  knitting needles
· Darning needle

CRAFT TIME

· 8 hours

Karolien Van de Gaer of Studio Meez is an independent
designer and artist based in Ghent, Belgium. Her work
encompasses graphic design, photography, textile design
and art. Karolien's pattern is for a pair of teeny tiny
mittens that will fit most babies aged 12 to 18 months.
It should be loosely knitted and can be made using any
colours you choose.

NOTE

If you are a beginner knitter,
you can find out how to do the
stitches on pages 128–33, and
find a list of abbreviations on
page 138.

CUFF

Using 2.25-mm (US 1) needles, cast on 52 stitches in B. Place the stitch marker and join in the round, being careful not to twist the stitches. Knit 1 round.

Round 1: *K1, p1, repeat * to the end. Work in rib stitch until work measures 3.8 cm (1½ in).

Next round: Change to 3.25-mm (US 3) needles and A. Repeat the following 6 rounds 4 times to make the pattern.

Round 1: Knit.

R2: *K1 in A, k1 in C, repeat*.

R3: *K1 in A, k1 in C, repeat*.

R4: Knit in A.

R5: *K1 in C, k1 in A, repeat*

R6: *K1 in C, k1 in A, repeat*

SHAPE MITTEN TOP
Knit 3 rounds in B.

Next round (dec): K10, ssk, k1, k2tog, k21, ssk, k1, k2tog, knit to end. 48 sts.

Next round (dec): K9, ssk, k1, k2tog, k19, ssk, k1, k2tog, knit to end. 44 sts.

Next round (dec): K8, ssk, k1, k2tog, k17, ssk, k1, k2tog, knit to end. 40 sts.

Next round (dec): K7, ssk, k1, k2tog, k15, ssk, k1, k2tog, knit to end. 36 sts.

Next round (dec): K6, ssk, k1, k2tog, k13, ssk, k1, k2tog, knit to end. 32 sts.

Next round (dec): K5, ssk, k1, k2tog, k11, ssk, k1, k2tog, knit to end. 28 sts.

Next round (dec): K4, ssk, k1, k2tog, k9, ssk, k1, k2tog, knit to end. 24 sts.

Next round (dec): K3, ssk, k1, k2tog, k7, ssk, k1, k2tog, knit to end. 20 sts.

Next round (dec): K2, ssk, k1, k2tog, k5, ssk, k1, k2tog, knit to end. 16 sts.

Next round (dec): K1, ssk, k1, k2tog, k3, ssk, k1, k2tog, knit to end. 12 sts.

Next round (dec): Ssk, k1, k2tog, k1, ssk, k1, k2tog, k1. 8 sts.

FINISHING OFF

Thread the working yarn through the remaining stitches and secure. Make a 61-cm (24-in) braid with leftover yarn. Use the darning needle and matching yarn to attach the braid ends to the mitten cuffs.

Pattern notes

- Tension: 7 stitches to 2.5 cm (1 in) in stocking stitch, using 3.25-mm (US 3) needles. Adjust needle size if necessary to obtain the correct tension.

- Stitch guide:
Rib: *K1, P1, repeat*.
Ssk: slip slip knit.

Finished size

- Length 14 cm (5½ in), width 9 cm (3½ in)

Slip slip knit (SSK)

- Slip 1 stitch from the left needle with the right needle as if to knit. Slip the next stitch on the left needle with the right needle as if to knit. Knit these two stitches together by inserting the left needle into the two slipped stitches from the left so that the right needle is positioned behind the left needle.

Knit 2 together (k2tog)

This creates a right-slanting decrease.

- Put the needle through the next two stitches on the left needle.

- Knit both stitches.

- Pull the yarn through both stitches and drop them off the left needle.

Once-a-year photobook

This gorgeous keepsake photo book was created by Australian designer, Josephine Palmer, for her company Laikonik. With space for a photograph each year until the age of 18, or for every week of the first four months, you can cherish all the changes that happen along the way in a child's life. The clever concertina design means you can stand and display it or fold and store it in a sleeve or bound with a ribbon. While Laikonik screenprints its own fabric, as shown here, you could use any lightweight fabric for the book cover.

YOU WILL NEED

For the book cover:
- Glue stick (acid-free)
- Two pieces of heavyweight box board or card, cut to 15 x 15 cm (6 x 6 in)
- 2 pieces of lightweight fabric for the front and back cut to about 17 x 17 cm (6¾ x 6¾ in) square
- Bone folder (or blunt butter knife)
- Scissors
- Pencil
- Steel ruler

For the inside pages:
- A0 sheet of heavyweight (300 to 380 gsm) acid-free paper (paper that is not acid free gradually disintegrates)
- Paperweight

CRAFT TIME

- 4 hours

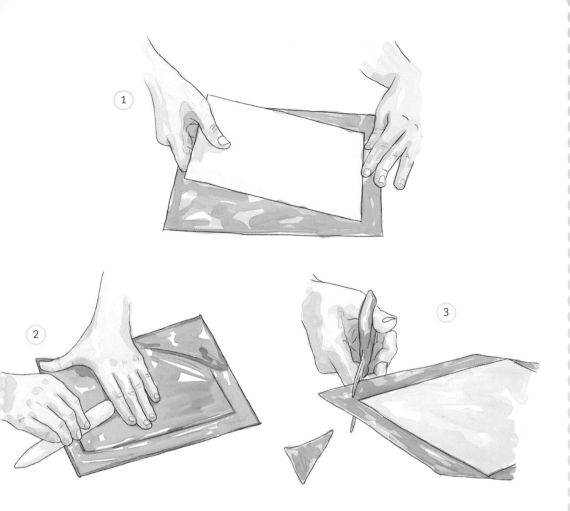

1. To make the cover, apply a generous amount of glue to one piece of box board. Carefully place the book board in the centre of a piece of fabric and press down.

2. Use a bone folder to smooth out any imperfections, such as air bubbles or ripples.

3. With scissors, trim the four corners of the book cloth along the diagonal, using the box board as a guide. Apply glue to the four sides of the box board where you will stick down the folded-over fabric.

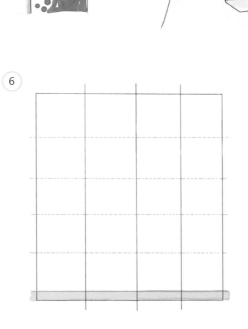

(4a)

(4b)

(6)

4. Lift one edge of the fabric and press it on to the back of the board (a). Use the bone folder to smooth and secure it (b). Repeat for all four sides. Tap the corners with the flat of the bone folder so they are not too pointed.

5. Repeat Steps 1–4 so you have two hard covers.

6. To make the pages, mark off an area measuring 60 x 91 cm (24 x 36 in) on your sheet of A0 paper. Use a pencil and ruler to divide the marked area into four sections across the page and five sections down the page. Measure three long panels across the page (15 x 91 cm/6 x 36 in) and one shorter panel (15 x 60 cm/6 x 24 in).

7. Mark fold lines every 15 cm (6 in) along each panel to make the concertina folders. Cut along the pink lines in the diagram for Step 6. Score (fold) along the blue dashed lines in a concertina/accordion style, using a blunt knife and ruler. The blue area at the bottom indicates the glue flap (the join). Note that the last panel does not need a glue fold.

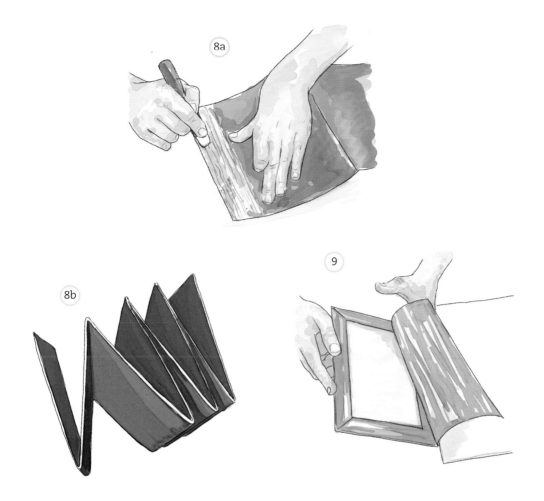

8. To connect all the five-page accordion units together, use the glue flap at the bottom (a). You will have 22 pages, including the two cover pages (b).

9. Glue the front and back covers onto the ends of the accordion unit. Fold flat. Rest a paperweight on the book and leave it for 30 minutes until the glue has set.

10. Now you can get creative! You could make an introductory page where you can fill in details such as place and date of birth, weight and height, and customise the cover however you like. You can add photos of your baby each year with details of their funny moments and precious anecdotes. This book chronicles your child from birth to adulthood.

Inspiration gallery

Left: These mini crown hats from Maker*Land are scaled-down versions of a full-size hat. Crowns can be made from different fabrics too.

Below left: These simple but sweet grey felt mittens by Studio Vlijt are hand-cut from two pieces of felt and sewn with a blanket stitch in a contrasting colour.

Below right: Using organic cotton loopback jersey, these thick and super-comfy spotty leggings were handmade by Kerstin Steger of Paul & Paula. She screenprinted simple copper spots on to them, perfect for little movers.

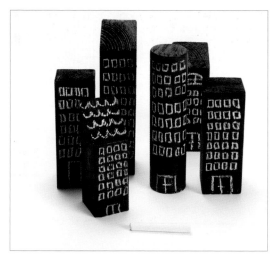

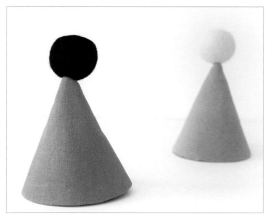

Above left: These blocks by Jenni Juurinen were painted with blackboard paint, so older babies can decorate them with their own drawings.

Above right: These beautifully soft harem pants by Abbie Wynot of Maisie Jayne are made of cotton elastane for comfort and fit. Able to stretch over even the largest of nappies, cloth or otherwise, they make the perfect baby trousers.

Middle left: Using Liberty Tana Lawn fabric, these bloomers were made by Paola Cattaneo of La Casetta in Canada from a pattern in *Intemporels pour bébés*. With an elasticated waist and legs they are perfect for a crawler or walker.

Left: Made using 100% pure linen, these birthday hats by Colette Bream feature a woollen pompom.

Resources: Knitting basics

Knitting is a skill that takes some time and practice to master. Here we go over the terms and basic techniques used in the knitted booties pattern on page 52, which is a great project for a beginner.

CAST-ON (LONG-TAIL METHOD)

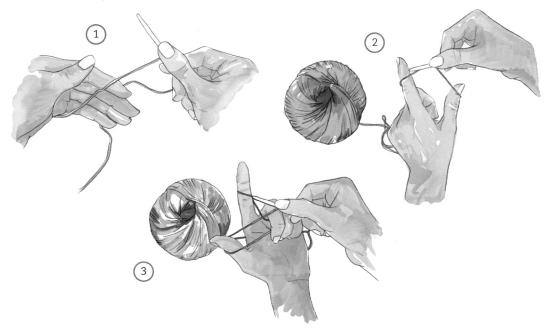

1. Position yarn over needle so that the tail is to the front, and the ball is to the back. For this project, allow yourself about 61 cm (24 in) of tail.

2. Hold yarn in place on the needle with your right thumb, insert left index finger and thumb between the two lengths of yarn, and grip with remaining fingers on left hand.

3. Pivot left hand so palm faces up and spread index finger and thumb apart.

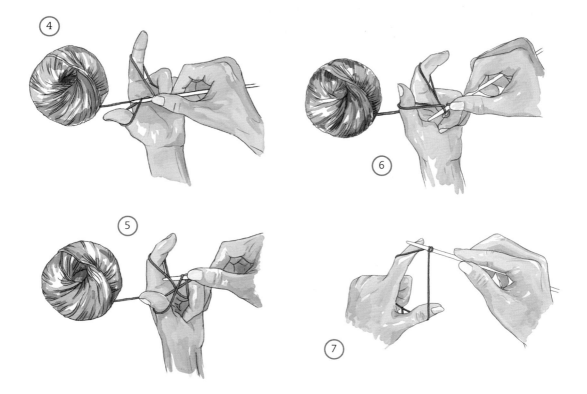

4. Move needle towards you over the taut yarn and pick up the yarn wrapped around the thumb, snagging it from the base of the thumb in an upwards motion.

5. Move needle away from you towards the index finger and pick up the yarn wrapped around the index finger, snagging it from behind in a forwards motion toward you.

6. Continue moving the needle forwards through the yarn you picked up on the thumb. Drop the loop around the thumb and gently pull both yarn lengths so that the yarn is snug on the needle.

7. You now have two stitches on the needle. Repeat Steps 2–5, casting on one new stitch with each repeat until you have the desired number of stitches.

KNIT

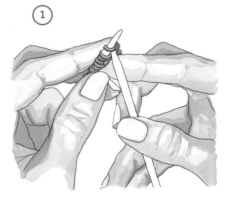

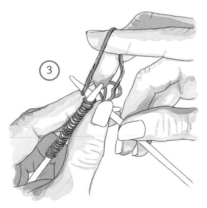

1. Holding the needle with the cast-on stitches in the left hand and second needle in the right hand. Insert the right needle through the first stitch from the left of the stitch.

2. With ball-side yarn held to the back of the work, move the right needle under the left needle through the stitch and hold it so the needles create an 'X'.

3. Take the ball-side yarn between the two needles, wrapping it around the right needle from behind.

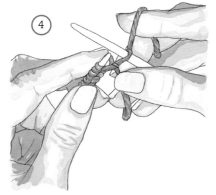

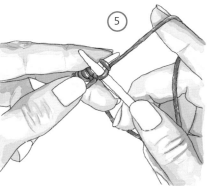

4. Slide the right needle back through the first stitch, carrying the ball-side yarn forwards with it.

5. Drop the first stitch off the left needle. You now have one new stitch on the right needle. Repeat Steps 1–5 to the end of the row.

PURL

①

②

③

④

1. Hold the needle with the cast-on stitches in the left hand, the second needle in the right hand, and the ball-side yarn held to the front of the work. Insert the right needle through the first stitch from the right of the stitch so the needles create an 'X'.

2. Take the ball-side yarn between the two needles and wrap it around the right needle from behind, right to left.

3. Slide the right needle back through the first stitch, carrying the ball-side yarn back with it.

4. Drop the first stitch off the left needle. You now have one new stitch on the right needle. Repeat Steps 1–4 to the end of the row.

Resources: Crochet basics

Crochet is a skill that takes some time and practice to learn but once you have mastered the techniques it is relatively easy and fast. The crochet baby blanket and crochet teether projects found on pages 54 and 88 are both great projects for beginners; the crochet baby blanket makes the best first project. If you are a complete beginner, it is recommended that you practise the basic stitches before you start.

CHAIN (CH)

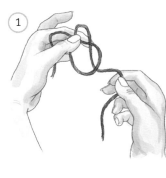

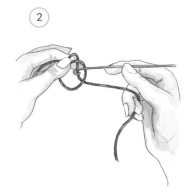

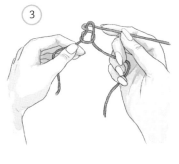

Crochet patterns usually begin with a series of chain stitches. This is called a foundation chain.

1. Make a loop with the yarn, with the short end to the left and the ball of yarn to the right (vice versa if you are left handed).

2. Take your hook in your right hand if you are right handed (or left if you are left handed), insert it through the loop, and catch the long end of the thread.

3. Pull the yarn through the loop with the hook. Pull the short and long ends of the yarn away from one another until the loop closes around your hook. This is a slip knot.

To chain, hold the hook in your right hand and the long piece of yarn (ball end) in your left. Switch hands if you are left handed. Take the hook under the yarn so that there is a loop of yarn over the front of the hook (yo). Pull the yarn through your slip knot to make a chain stitch. Repeat as many times as the pattern requires.

SLIP STITCH (SL ST)

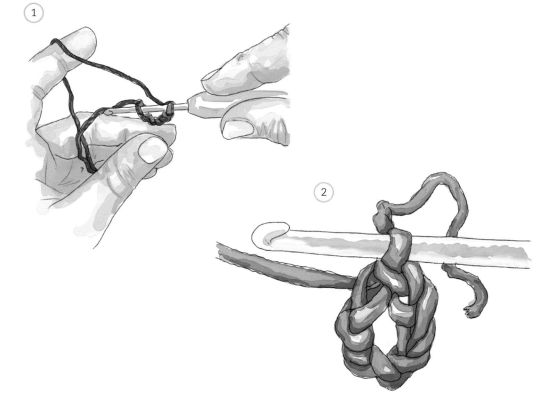

This stitch is often used for joining stitches together. Here we show you how to use it to join a chain to make a ring.

1. Working with a base of 6 chain stitches, insert the hook into the first chain stitch from front to back. You will have the stitch and the original loop on the hook.

2. Catch the yarn, take it over the hook (yo), and pull it through the stitch and the original loop. This is a slip stitch.

DOUBLE CROCHET (DC)

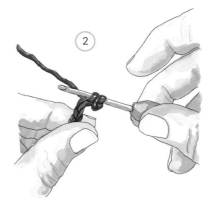

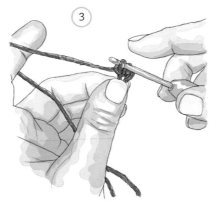

To practise this stitch, first make a chain of 12 stitches.

1. Insert the hook into the third chain from the hook, catch the yarn and take it over the hook (yo).

2. Pull the yarn through so there are two loops on your hook.

3. Catch the yarn again (yo) and pull through both loops. This is a double crochet stitch.

TREBLE CROCHET (TC)

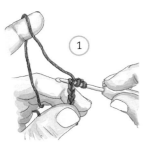

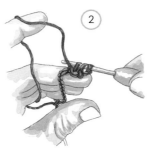

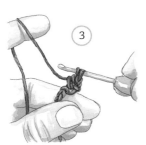

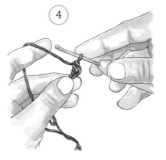

Starting a new ball of yarn

If your yarn runs out, simply take your new ball, tie the ends together and carry on crocheting. You can weave in the two ends later.

Finishing off

Once you have completed the final stitch on the pattern, cut the yarn around 10–12 cm (4–5 in) from the end. Pull through the loop on your hook and tighten to secure. Using a blunt-tipped yarn needle, weave the ends into the back of your work. Weave in the end in one direction, then weave back over it in the other direction to make sure it is secure. Cut off the excess yarn. This is also how you weave in any excess yarn on your work after adding in a new ball of yarn or changing colour.

To practise this stitch, first make a chain of 12 stitches.

1. Take the yarn over the hook (yo) and insert the hook into the third chain from the hook. You will have two loops and the stitch on your hook.

2. Catch the yarn over the hook and pull through the stitch. You will have three loops on your hook.

3. Catch the yarn over the hook (yo) and pull through the first two loops. You will now have two loops on your hook.

4. Catch the yarn over the hook again (yo) and pull through both loops. This is a treble crochet stitch.

Abbreviations & glossary

CROCHET

ch	chain
ss or sl st	slip stitch
dc	double crochet
tc	treble crochet
dc2tog	double crochet 2 together
rep	repeat
sk	skip
yo	yarn over

KNITTING

( )	alternate instructions for size or measurement within parentheses.
[ ]	repeat the instructions between the brackets as many times as is indicated directly after them.
K	knit
K2tog	knit 2 together
K2tog tbl	knit 2 together through back loop
P	purl
patt	pattern
rep or *	repeat
RS	right side
ssk	slip slip knit
st	stitch
WS	wrong side
yo	yarn over

backstitch
Stitches are sewn backwards in the direction of sewing. This is a strong stitch that is more secure than running/straight stitch.

baste
To sew together temporarily with removable stitches.

blanket stitch
See whip stitch

ladder stitch
Invisible stitch used to join folded edges of fabric together, for instance, to close a hole after turning an item such as a pillowcase the right way out.

raw edge
Unfinished or cut edge of fabric.

running stitch
Also known as straight stitch, this commonly used stitch is a basic sewing stitch.

straight stitch
See running stitch

whip stitch
Also known as blanket stitch, this stitch is good for neatening up edges by hand.

zigzag stitch
This machine stitch is good for neatening up the edges of seams.

Contributor index

PHOTOGRAPHY CREDITS

Index

Acknowledgements

This book would not have been possible if it wasn't for the hard work of all the different crafters and makers from around the world who dedicated their time and creative energies to us and made these special projects for the book.

We'd like to thank, in no particular order: Zeena Shah, Audrey Smit, Allyssa Zemke, Delia Randall, Jessica Kelly, Crystal Motes, Michelle Kreussel, Jana Klocková Kudrnová, Mandy Pellegrin, Eri Flores, Rae Anne Spence, Courtney Spainhower, Andrea Hanki, Shannon Lamden, Lainie Wicks, An Kuppens, Sanae Shida, Minhee Cho, Kristen Bach, Sarmite Strautina, Dace Seglina-Grinblate, Jenni Juurinen, Karolien Van de Gaer and Josephine Palmer.

Thank you also to those who created examples of their work to be included in each of the inspiration galleries.

Finally, a very special thanks to the editorial team at RotoVision for their support throughout the making of this book, in particular, Isheeta Mustafi, Tamsin Richardson and Cath Senker.

Charlotte Rivers and Emily Gregory